Introduction to iPad and iPhone

The Photos App

iOS/iPadOS 16 Edition

© 2023 iTandCoffee

Who is iTandCoffee?

iTandCoffee is an Australian-based small business established in 2012, offering technology support and education – for personal and small business technology. Our books are generally have corresponding classes and videos on the same topic.

The focus of iTandCoffee has always been on providing patient, friendly and supportive assistance – acknowledging that technology is a daunting and mystifying subject for so many people.

While iTandCoffee has always had a strong focus on Apple devices, we also provide assistance with, and training on, a wide range of other technology topics, including Android, Windows, Microsoft 365 and other cloud products, and much more – for home, and in business.

iTandCoffee operates in and around Camberwell, Victoria (in Australia), and also offers support and training remotely - both nationally and worldwide.

Visit www.itandcoffee.com.au to learn more about iTandCoffee.

Subscribe to the iTandCoffee newsletter at www.itandcoffee.com.au/newsletter.

Become an iTandCoffee member at www.itandcoffee.com.au/itandcoffee-club.

iTandCoffee Products and Services

For queries about iTandCoffee products and services – including our books, videos, newsletter, appointments, classes, membership and more - call **1300 885 420** (Australia only) or email **enquiry@itandcoffee.com.au**.

Introduction to the iPad and iPhone

The Photos App

TABLE OF CONTENTS

TABLE OF CONTENTS

TABLE OF CONTENTS

TABLE OF CONTENTS

TABLE OF CONTENTS

Before we start

Introducing the term 'thumbnail' ...

A **thumbnail** is the term used to describe a miniature version of a picture or video. The below image shows 'thumbnails' of some old photos, displayed with a square aspect ratio. (We talk about aspect ratio on page 24 and on page 83.)

Thumbnails are used in the Photos app to help in recognising and organising photos and videos, by giving a preview of a set of photos. Various options are then available for managing the photos that appear in this thumbnail view.

Important Finger Gestures

When using the Photos app, there are some important finger gestures to learn.

The usual quick **tap** means 'select'. In the above screen, tapping on any of the thumbnails will show a larger view of that individual photo. (Note that all taps are with the pad of the finger, not with the fingernail.)

But there is another powerful gesture that works in several places.

Before we start

It is the **touch and hold** gesture – i.e. placing your finger on, say, a thumbnail and holding it there. After about a second, a menu of options will appear, as shown in the image on the right.

This touch and hold gesture also works in lots of other places in the Photos App – which we will cover throughout this book.

In fact, this gesture works in lots of places on your iPad & iPhone.

We will also refer to **zooming** using two fingers in a pinch, then spread outwards (and vice versa).

Pinching outwards will expand the image/s in view.

Pinching inwards after doing this will reduce the Zoom.

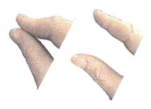

In some places, pinching inwards will return you to the previous view.

The term 'metadata'

In a few different places in this document, we will refer to the term 'metadata'.

Metadata is the information stored about a photo – where it was taken, when, with what camera/device, file size, a caption, resolution, and more.

We will look at how view (and perhaps modify) to metadata associated with your photos.

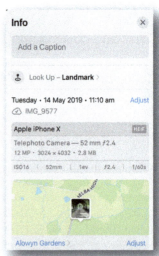

About the Photos App

The Photos app on the iPad and iPhone lets you view and manage photos and videos that you capture on, or import to, your iPad or iPhone.

Your photos are stored in 'albums', some of which are standard albums provided by Apple. You can then also create your own custom Albums, to help you to organise your photos (which we cover from page 59).

The **Photos** App also gives the option of viewing your photos in date order (regardless of what album they are stored in.

This is the **Library** option in the menu bar at bottom on the iPhone and at the top of the left sidebar on iPad. It gives a 'timeline' of your photos according to the date the 'Date Taken' metadata of the photo. We cover the Library view in detail from page 21.

There is also a **For You** option, providing slideshows and collections of photos that are created for you, using your own photos - on a range of topics like 'In Nature', 'Home', 'On This Day', 'Best of Last Week' and more. We look at on this section a from page 38.

Also available are views of your photos by People, Places, Media Type and more.

About the Photos App

Your other iPad/iPhone applications can use your photos/videos and albums that are stored in your **Photos** library - for example, when inserting a photo in an email, the search screen allows you to browse **Photos** for the image you wish to include.

It is important to understand that, while a particular photo may appear under more than one 'album' or in more than one of the library areas in Photos, that each photo **exists only once in the library** (unless you deliberately create a duplicate – see page 93).

When you add a photo or video to an album, **you are not moving it or copying it**. We'll talk about this in more detail throughout this guide.

But let's first take a bit of a Guided Tour of the Photos app on both the iPad and iPhone.

A Guided Tour of the Photos App

As you will have no doubt noticed, the 'look' of the Photos app on the iPad and iPhone is quite different.

We will look iPad – at the main areas and options – and also note where to find the each of these on the iPhone.

The Sidebar

Let's look first at the Sidebar on the left of the Photos app on the iPad, which is indicated with a red box in the image below.

The main sections in the Photos sidebar on the iPad are Photos, Utilities, Media Types, Shared Albums and My Albums.

The same areas are also available on the iPhone, but just located differently.

Before we start, it is important to note that the detail of each section in the iPad sidebar can be hidden.

If you are only seeing the name of any section and not its contents – as shown in the example on the right – tap the > to expand the section.

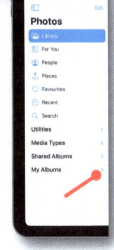

A Guided Tour of the Photos App

In the same way, you can hide the contents of each section by hovering over the section name and tapping the symbol ⌄.

If you do not see the iPad sidebar at all, tap the symbol indicated in the image on the right (which is found at top left in the main view of the Photos app) to make it appear again.

Tap that same symbol to hide the sidebar.

Photos

The top section of the sidebar is Photos, which provides several options for viewing your photos, each of which we will cover in more detail in subsequent pages.

Library   View your whole photos library as timeline, based on 'Date Taken'.
In Library view, options along the top allow you to choose different ways to view this full collection of photos:

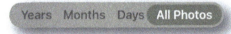

Years	View your photos grouped by Year
Months	View your photos grouped by Month
Day	View your photos grouped by Day
All Photos	View your timeline of all photos by date/time

For the iPhone, this option is found in the bottom bar, leftmost option. (More about Library from page 21

For You   The Photos app will automatically create 'curated collections' of your photos, to help you re-discover forgotten memories buried in your photos, see photos that it chooses to feature, see photos that have been **Shared with You** by others (in Messages), and more.

A Guided Tour of the Photos App

Visit this option regularly to see your new 'Memories' and other curated content. (More details from page 38.)

For the iPhone, this option is found in the bottom bar, second option from the left.

People

The Photos app helps you identify and group photos of people, so that you can view collections of photos for the various people in your life.

For the iPhone, this option is under **Albums** (third option along the bottom bar) – scroll down to the **People and Places** section. (See page 45 for more on People).

Places

View your photos on a map, based on the location that was recorded against the photo when it was taken.

Zoom in and out on this map to 'split out' your photos by their location. It is a great way of seeing all the places you have been! (See Page 43 for more details.)

For the iPhone, this option is under **Albums** (third option along the bottom bar) – scroll down to the **People and Places** section.

Favourites

View those photos you have marked as your 'Favourites'. (See page 26 for more details.)

For the iPhone, this option under **Albums** (third option along the bottom bar). It is in the **My Albums** section (first section), directly under the **Recent** thumbnail.

Recent

Your photos listed in the order in which they were added to your Photos library. So, if you just saved a photo to your library from, say, an email, it will appear as the last photo – even it that photo was taken a while ago. (See page 27 for more details.)

For the iPhone, this option under **Albums** (third option along the bottom bar). It is in the **My Albums** section and is the first thumbnail in that section.

Search

Search for photos based on all sorts of search criteria like place, person, photo content (e.g. search for all photos with a beach, or with a dog), words in captions, date and more. (See page 94 for more details.)

For the iPhone, this is the rightmost option in the bottom bar.

A Guided Tour of the Photos App

Utilities

Imports
Imports allows you to view your photos according to when they were imported to your Photos library. Imports could be from places like emails, a camera, or an external storage device. (See page 98 for details of how to save from Mail, Messages and Safari, and page 101 for further details on importing from a camera.)

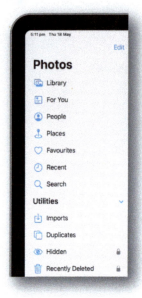

For the iPhone, this option is under **Albums** (third option along the bottom bar) – scroll down to the **Utilities** section, and it is the first option you see there.

Duplicates
View and manage the photos that have been identified as Duplicates. This can be on a case-by-case basis or select all in this area and choose to merge all duplicates in one go. (See page 105 for further details.)

For the iPhone, this option is under **Albums** (third option along the bottom bar) – scroll down to the **Utilities** section, and it is the second option you see there.

Hidden
This album will only appear if you have chosen to Hide any of your photos from the other views. This is handy for photos that you don't really want other to see. I used it to hide screenshots that I was taking of regular Speed Tests of my internet, which I don't want clogging up my Timeline and other views. (See page 29 and 31 for further details.)

For the iPhone, this option is under **Albums** (third option along the bottom bar) – scroll down to the **Utilities** section, and it is the third option you see there.

Recently Deleted
Deleted photos are moved to this area and retained for around 30 days, after which they are deleted. (See Page 30 and 31 for further details.)

For the iPhone, this option is under **Albums** (third option along the bottom bar) – scroll down to the **Utilities** section, and it is the fourth option you see there.

A Guided Tour of the Photos App

Media Types

This section groups your photos /videos according to their type – videos, selfies, live photos, etc.

Photos and videos will automatically appear in these albums based on their format/type.

You cannot choose what goes in these albums – and some albums will be missing if there are no photos/videos of that type in the library.

For the iPhone, this option is under **Albums** (third option along the bottom bar) – scroll down to the **Media Types** section.

Shared Albums

This section shows all the Shared Albums that have been shared with you via iCloud, or that you have shared with others.

This section will only appear if you have chosen to enable **Shared Albums** in your iCloud settings on the device. This is covered more fully a bit later, from page 118.

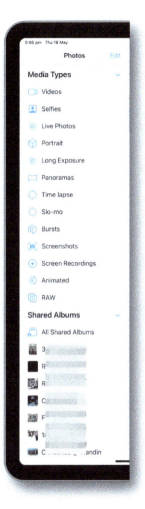

For the iPhone, this option is under **Albums** (third option along the bottom bar) – it is the second section in that area.

A Guided Tour of the Photos App

My Albums

This section shows all the Folders and Albums that you have created. The example on the right shows my set of Folders, under which are the Albums.

We'll look at how to create these a bit later – from page 59.

Choose the **All Albums** option to see Recent and Favourites (both of which are standard Albums from Apple, shown in the top section of the Sidebar as well), then each of your own Albums/Folders shown as thumbnails. Under All Albums will be your list of Folders and Albums you have created.

For the iPhone, the **My Albums** option is under **Albums** (third option along the bottom bar) – and is the very first section in that area.

Toolbar options

In most views of the Photos app, you will notice a set of symbols located in various places, depending on whether you are looking at the iPad or iPhone – and depending on your current view.

Let's look at the meaning of these symbols – we'll then cover these things in more detail later.

Show information about the photo that is currently selected. This information includes the camera it was taken with, when it was taken, its size, location, and perhaps the people in it. For some photos (e.g. of dogs, plants, flowers, etc), this information may include additional information about the subject - in which case there will stars at top left of the ⓘ.

Share a photo (or set of photos) – for example, via Messages, Mail or Airdrop.

A Guided Tour of the Photos App

 Flag a photo (or several photos) as being a 'favourite' – these photos then appear in the Favourites area.

 Delete the photo. It will be sent to Recently Deleted area and disappear from other library views.

 Edit the currently visible individual photo – including cropping, rotating, brightening and lots more.

 Shows on the iPad at top right, in views that show thumbnails of photos – allowing the Aspect Ratio of the photos in the view to be changed between Square and Aspect. Square looks better but doesn't show the true orientation of the photo. On the iPhone, this option can be chosen from the More Options menu (⋯) (covered below)

 Appears in views that show photo thumbnails, allowing for the selection (by tapping) of a set of photos for which some action is required (e.g. Delete, Add to an Album, Share, etc).

 Provides more options for the selected photo (left image below) or for the set of photos in view (right image below).

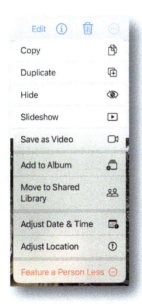
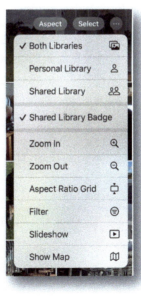

A Guided Tour of the Photos App

The Albums Option on the iPhone

We have already mentioned the iPhone's **Albums** view in earlier descriptions, but let's just take a quick look at it at what it looks like before we go any further.

The **Albums** view is broken into several main sections:

- **My Albums** – same content as show unter the My Albums section of the iPad Sidebar
- **Shared Albums** – same content as show unter the Shared Albums section of the iPad Sidebar
- **People and Places** – as the name suggests, contains the People and Places albums, the same albums as found in the top section of the left sidebar on the iPad
- **Media Types** – same content as described above for the Media Types section of the iPad sidebar
- **Utilities** – same content as described above for the Utilities section of the iPad sidebar

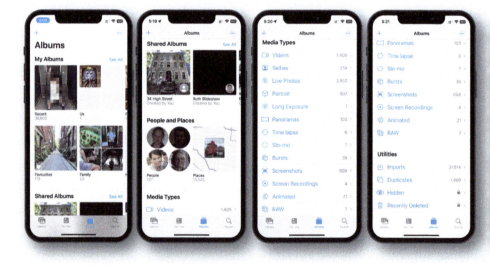

The Library Option

A Timeline of your Photos

Years   Months   Days   All Photos

When you tap on the **Library** option in the menu bar at the bottom on the iPhone or at the top of the sidebar on the iPad, you will see your photos ordered according to their 'date taken' – and perhaps grouped in one of three ways.

In the Library view, photos can be viewed in a summarized form, by **Years, Months,** and **Days**. Or **All Photos** can be viewed, listed in date order.

On the iPhone, tap the bar along the bottom to choose how to view your Library.

On the iPad, this same bar is along the top.

It shows all the options described above – Years, Months, Days, All Photos.

The Library Option

Years

Years Months Days All Photos

The **Years** view shows large 'thumbnails' of each the years that are represented by your collection of photos, according to each photo's 'date taken'.

(Note. We'll cover later how you can adjust this 'date taken' so that photos with incorrect dates – e.g. scanned old photos – appear in the correct place on this timeline, as demonstrated in the image on the right.)

Tap on any of these thumbnails to view the photos represented by that year, grouped by month.

Months

Years Months Days All Photos

Months view provides a summary of photos, listed in Month order – with large thumbnails to represent collections of photos within each month.

Tap on any of these large thumbnails to view the associated photos.

Tap the symbol ● at top right of the thumbnail. You will see the options:

- **Share Photos** to share the set of photos with others (we'll look at sharing options later
- **Play Memory Movie** to view a slideshow (with music) of the set of photos or
- **Show Map** to view the set of photos on a map (if any location metadata is available for the photos)

The Library Option

(Note. You may not see all these three options. It depends on the photos in the Month.)

To see all the photos associated with the month and surrounding months, tap the **All Photos** option when you have the applicable month in view.

Days

The **Days** view provides a summarised view of the day's photos in a 'gallery' format'. It won't necessarily show all the photos for that day.

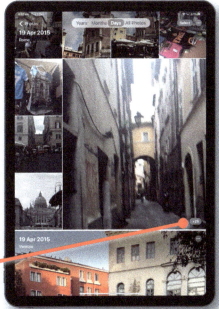

Tap on any **thumbnail** of a photo in your **Days** view to view that individual photo.

To see all the photos associated with that day and surrounding days, tap the **All Photos** option when you have the applicable date in view.

If you see a number in an oval at the bottom right of a thumbnail (as shown right), this means there are further photos associated that day. Tap the number to view those photos.

Touch and hold on any photo thumbnail to see a menu of options that apply to the selected photo (see right).

23

The Library Option

All Photos

The **All Photos** view allows for the viewing of all photos by 'date taken'. Tap **All Photos** at any point while scrolling Years, Months and Days to see all the photos associated with your current point in the timeline.

Pinch inwards and outwards to zoom the photo thumbnails in and out.

As shown below, the thumbnails can be made very small, to allow you to scan for a point in time and photo.

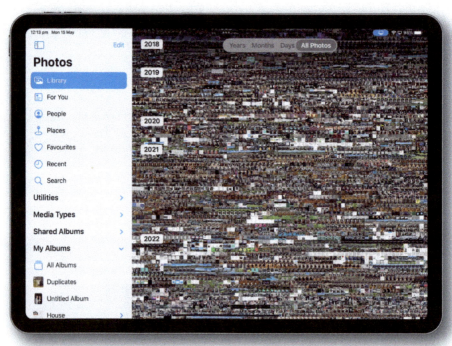

Choose the Aspect Ratio

When viewing all your photos in the **All Photos** view (or in Albums), choose whether to view **Square** or **Aspect** (true proportions) thumbnails.

On the iPad, the option will appear at the top right if the thumbnails are a reasonable size.

The Library Option

Below left is **Square** view – in which case the **Aspect** option shows at top right of that screen, to allow the switch to that view. Below right is the **Aspect** view, and the **Square** option now shows at top right (to allow the switch to Square view).

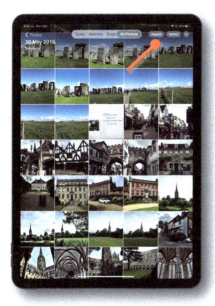 

On the iPhone, tap the 'More Options' symbol to see the option **Aspect Ratio Grid** or **Square Photo Grid** (depending on the current view).

Other options for viewing your Photos Library

People   ⊙ People

We'll cover this one in a more detailed from page 45.

Places   ⚲ Places

We'll cover this one in a more detailed from page 43.

Favourites   ♡ Favourites

Favourites is a special album that shows any photos you've marked as being your Favourites – by tapping the Heart symbol. ♡

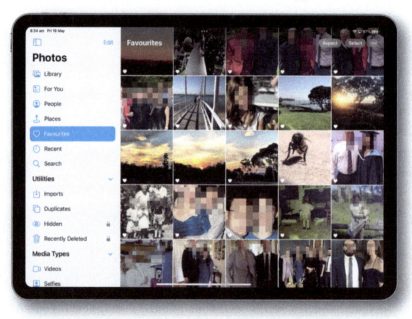

Your Favourite photos can be selected in a number of ways:

- In individual photo view, by tapping the heart icon at the bottom ♡ (iPhone) or top (iPad) when viewing the individual photo.

- In photo thumbnail view, by touching and holding on a photo's thumbnail and choosing the **Favourite** option.

- In photo thumbnail view, by tapping **Select** at top right, tapping to tick/select the photos you wish to favor, then choosing ⋯ at bottom right, then tapping the **Favourite** option.

Other options for viewing your Photos Library

To remove a favourite, just tap on it (or on several) and tap the heart symbol in the toolbar at top right. The 'un-favoured' photos will disappear from the Favourites view.

If you use iCloud to sync your Photos, the same set of Favourites will appear across all your devices – i.e. they will sync.

If you are not using iCloud Photos (covered from page 107), **Favourites** you have chosen on your iPad or iPhone are separate to those on your Mac and vice-versa. This means that, even if you have 'hearted' a photo on your iPhone, it won't automatically appear in Favourites on your Mac (or your iPad, for that matter).

Recent   ⏱ Recent

The **Recent** view lists your photos according to date they 'arrived' in the Photo library.

This means that the order you see here may be different to that you see in the **Library** (timeline) views described earlier, since a photo taken several years ago but just saved to Photos will appear as the last photo in Recent.

To see any photo from the **Recent** view in its 'date' order (and with other photos taken on the same or adjacent dates), touch and hold on the photo thumbnail in **Recent** and choose **Show in All Photos**.

Other options for viewing your Photos Library

Imports

The Imports view in Library shows the photos according to the date they were imported to your Mac from a Camera, SD Card, iPhone or iPad, or any another import method – see later in this guide for methods of importing photos you your Photos library.

If you want to quickly move a set of photos imported on a particular date to an Album – or perhaps delete them (or some other action) – tap **Select** at top right.

You will then see, for each group of imported photos, a **Select** option on the right side – allowing you to select that set of photos. Once selected, choose then to Share, Delete, Add to Album, and more (which we will cover in more detail soon).

Other options for viewing your Photos Library

Hidden   Hidden

The **Hidden** album includes any photos you have chosen to **Hide** from the casual observer!

Photos that you Hide are not shown in other Library views.

To Hide a photo that you see in a thumbnail view, **touch and hold** on the photo and choose **Hide.**

When viewing the individual photo, tap the ⊙ at top right and choose **Hide.**

Photos then lets you then choose whether the **Hidden** album appears in the Photos app.

Go to the **Settings** app, scroll down to the **Photos** option and turn off **Show Hidden Album** if you don't want to see the Hidden album in the library.

Note that you will still be able to choose to Hide photos.

Come back to this Setting to turn on the the Hidden Album if ever you need to look at and manage the set of photos there.

Touch and hold on any photo that is in the Hidden album and choose **Unhide** to return that photo to the main Photos views.

With iOS/iPadOS 16, you can also choose to protect this Hidden album, requiring authentication to view it (if it is visible).

Turn on the **Use Face ID** (or **Use Touch ID** or **Use Passcode**) switch above **Show Hidden Album** to enable this authentication (which applies to the **Recently Deleted** album as well).

Other options for viewing your Photos Library

Recently Deleted

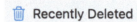

Just as it sounds, the **Recently Deleted** album holds photos you have decided to 'trash'.

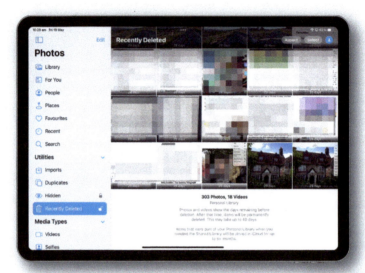

The Photos App retains deleted photos and videos for about 30 days (sometimes up to 40 days) in case you make a mistake and need to retrieve them.

Photos in this album show the days remaining before permanent deletion.

To permanently delete the photos from this album (and thereby free up their allocated storage), just choose the **Select** option at top right, then **Delete All** (which will be at bottom left after choosing Select).

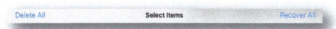

Alternatively, if you find you have deleted a photo or video in error, just select **Recently Deleted**, tap Select and tap the applicable photo/s (a tick will appear at bottom right), and choose the **Recover** option at bottom right.

Other options for viewing your Photos Library

New for Hidden and Deleted Albums in iOS/iPadOS 16

The Hidden and Deleted albums are now protected by your Face/Touch ID and your passcode, so that you can be sure that there is no unauthorised access to the photos in this area.

When you tap on either of these albums, you will now see an authentication screen appear – asking you to provide Face/Touch ID authentication (or your Passcode if neither of these is set up or your face/touch is not recognised).

Only after authentication will the content of the album appear.

If you don't require such protection for these albums, go to the Settings app - to **Settings -> Photos.**

Turn off the **Use Face ID** setting (which may be labelled **Use Touch ID** or **Use Passcode**, depending on which method of authentication is being used).

Viewing individual photos

When you are in a view that shows the individual photo thumbnails (for example, the All Photos view shown below left) tap on any image's thumbnail to view that individual photo.

The strip of tiny photos at the bottom of the screen will show the photo that is currently selected and the 'surrounding' photos.

Swipe from right to left on the screen (and vice versa) to move through these photos.

Or tap on any of the other tiny thumbnails on the strip at the bottom to jump to the photo.

You can also drag this strip one way or the other to quickly move between the photos shown.

You will find that, when you initially view the individual photo, there are bars at the top and bottom of the screen (showing the various options and the strip of photos).

Tap on the screen to make these bars go away and see your photo in full-screen mode, without any of these distractions.

Then, simply tap the screen again to make the bars and options re-appear.

Viewing individual photos

Use the < on the top left to go 'back up' to the previous level.

See more about your photo

When viewing an individual photo, **slide upwards** to uncover some additional options for that photo.

Alternatively, press the ⓘ at top right on the iPad, bottom on iPhone.

See where the photo was taken, when it was taken, **Add a Caption** describing the photo (which is searchable), and more.

If your photo is of something like a plant or animal, you may see a **Look Up** section. Tap here to find out more about the 'thing' – for example, the type of plant, or the breed of dog.

For such photos that have the Look Up feature, the ⓘ symbol will have a star on it ⓘ - to indicate the availability of this extra information.

You will also notice that, if you are viewing the photo from view other than one of the Library views (e.g. if you are in Recent, People, Places, a Media Type Album or one of your own Albums), you will have the option to **Show in All Photos** – very handy when you want to see the current photo in the context of other photos taken around the same time.

Viewing individual photos

If your photo has any text – Live Text

If there is any text in the image that you are currently viewing, you may see (depending on the model of your iPhone/iPad) a little symbol at the bottom right. This symbol is the **Live Text** symbol, indicating that some text has been detected.

Tap the symbol to work with the text in the image – to Copy, Select All, Speak, Translate and more.

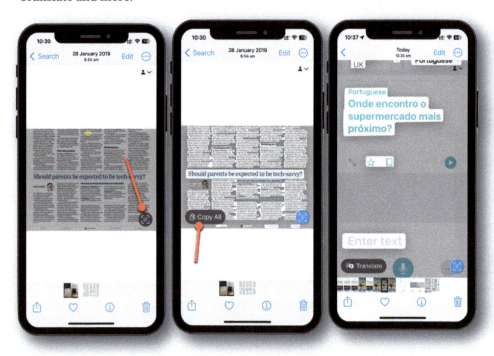

In the example in the left and middle images above, tapping the Live Text symbol selects all the text in the image of an article, and provides the **Copy All** to option on bottom left of the image – allowing all the article's text to be copied and then pasted elsewhere. Or I can use standard text selection techniques to select just some of the text to copy.

In the rightmost example above (which is a screenshot taken from the Translate app, containing a sentence in Portuguese), I see a **Translate** option   🌐 Translate
– which has appeared because the image contains text in a language other than my default language, allowing the quick translation (in this case) from Portuguese to English. Very handy when travelling!

Viewing individual photos

Viewing a Live photo

You may have a particular type of photo in your library, called a **Live** photo, available now in the Camera app on most iPhone and iPad models.

A **Live** photo is a photo that has a short video associated with it, showing the second or so before and after you took the photo – with audio.

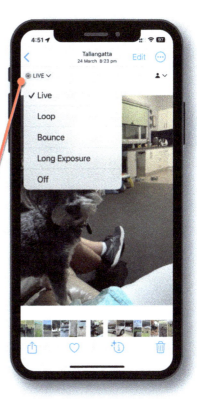

You can tell that a photo is a Live photo because it shows ◎ LIVE at the top left.

To view the video associated with the Live photo, simply hold your finger on the photo and watch it play.

Try different Live photo Effects

There are some fun things you can do with a Live photo.

Tap on the word **Live** at top left, and to see a list of options that can transform your Live photo.

Loop will play the short video on a continual loop.

Bounce will play the video forward, then backwards on a continual loop.

Long Exposure is great for shots like 'babbling brooks' – where you can get that lovely misty effect (see example on right).

If you choose the Loop or Bounce effect, your created videos will be found in the **Album** called **Animated** in the **Media Types** area.

Viewing individual photos

Lift a subject from a photo

A fun (and, for me, handy) new feature of iOS/iPadOS 16 is the ability to lift a subject from a picture – without the background.

I use this regularly when taking photos of things I want to use on my website or in books.

As an example, later in this book (on page 103) you will see an image that I created using this very feature.

I took a photo of a USB stick that I have (that can plug into both a computer and my iPad, that has both USB-A and USB-C ends to it).

On the left below is the photo that I took, and on the right is the photo that just has the object in it – without the background.

All I need to do to pull out the subject/object from an image like that above left is to touch my finger on the subject/object briefly (a little longer than the usual 'tap').

A glowing line gradually surrounds that object, showing that the object is being detected – and then the options to **Copy** or **Share** appear.

The **Share** option provides the option to **Save Image**, which saves the object as a separate photo – minus the background.

Or I can tap **Copy**, then paste the background-less object to a Message, an email, or elsewhere. Very handy!

Viewing individual photos

Play a video

If the item you have selected to view is a video, you will see a bar of controls at the top of the iPad and the bottom of the iPhone.

When the video is selected, the video will automatically start playing – and can be paused by tapping the ‖ symbol in this bar (shown in the iPad screen below left). (Note. In Settings -> Photos, you can disable this 'auto-play' feature if desired.)

To start the paused video, press the ▶ (as shown at the bottom of the iPhone screen on right).

The bar at the bottom shows the clips of the video you are viewing.

Tap on the video thumbnail in that bar, then drag the bar right and left to scan through the video's frames.

'Heart' your Favourites

You may have noticed that the bar of options that is visible when viewing individual photos includes the ♡ option. Tap this symbol to nominate the photo as a 'Favourites'.

The photo will then automatically appear in the **Favourites** album.

Any photo that has been set as a 'Favourite' will show a shaded heart. Just tap the heart again to 'unshade' it and remove the photo from your **Favourites** album.

'For You' —
Curated Collections of Photos

The **For You** option was introduced in late 2018, replacing the **Memorie**s option that was previously a main option. Memories is now just one of the many views provided in the **For You** option.

For You presents various 'curated' collections of your photos, under headings such as:

- Memories
- Featured Photos
- Recently Shared
- Shared Album Activity
- Sharing Suggestions
- Effect Suggestions

Not all of these headings will appear on the **For You** area, as their presence will depend on your previous 'sharing' activity, whether you have done any 'people' identification (covered a bit later) and the type of iPhone you have (and what features in includes). You can also turn off suggested content in this area from **Settings -> Photos**.

The order of these sections will also change.

It is well worth exploring **For You** to uncover some great photos and memories from amongst your photos.

'Memories'

The **For You** option provides a variety of collections of photos under the heading **Memories**.

The collections in the **Memories** area will be chosen for you automatically by the Photos app, from (supposedly) the best photos in the library - although I'm not convinced this is always true!

You may see Memories from a particular date, occasion, at a particular place, on someone's birthday, of a particular person through the years – and other 'topics.

'For You' -
Curated Collections of Photos

Tap on a **Memory** thumbnail to see a slideshow with music. Tap the screen to see some options for this slideshow.

Tap  at bottom right to see thumbnails of the photos in the Memory. Tap ♫ to change the music.

At top left is the 🔇 symbol for muting the music.

Pause the slideshow by tapping ⏸ then ▶ to re-start it.

Tap ⊙ at top right to see some further options for the Memory and its photos.

You could spend all day looking at your Memories!

If you like the Memory, you can choose to keep it – by adding it to your Favourites.

You will **Add To Favourites** by tapping ⊙ at top right when viewing the Memory (as shown in image on right).

Alternatively, tap the heart symbol that appears at the top right of the Memory thumbnail.

If you don't like that Memory, tap ⊙ at top right of the memory and choose **Delete Memory**.

You will also see the option to **Feature Less** and **Edit Title**.

'For You' -
Curated Collections of Photos

To view your Favourite memories, tap **See All** at top right of the **Memories** section of **For You**.

This will show a long list of memories. Tap [image] at the top right of that view, then tap the **Favourite Memories** option to view just those you have chosen as favourites.

When vieiwing only Favourites, tap that symbol and choose **All Memories** to see all again.

For further details on the Memory feature, check out the Apple Support article https://support.apple.com/en-au/HT207023.

Featured Photos

This section highlights photos which the app selects from your library – a random little collection again of photos for you to flick through.

I just did this on my own phone and found some lovely photo memories to share with others!

Shared with You

This section shows photos that others have shared with you via the Messages app.

Photos with a [image] symbol at bottom left are only in your Messages and have not yet been added to your Photos library.

Photos without this symbol are already in your Photos library.

To add those that are only in Messages, tap **Select** at top right, tap to tick the required photos, then tap [image] (bottom right) and **Save n Photos**.

'For You' - Curated Collections of Photos

Shared Albums Activity

Also in the **For You** view is **Shared Album Activity.**

This section relates to iCloud's Shared Albums, which we describe later in this guide, from page 118.

Visit this area to see who has posted comments or photos about albums you have shared, or that have been shared with you via iCloud.

Also shown here will be activity relating to any invitations you have sent for others to share your Albums via iCloud – or invitations to join someone else's Shared Album.

Swipe from right to left to see a summary of activity relating to each Shared Album.

Choose See All to see the history of all shared album activity back through time.

Sharing Suggestions

Sharing Suggestions offers a new way of sharing a collection of photos, without needing to set up Shared Albums via iCloud (described from page 118).

(Note. This feature is only available if you have turned on iCloud Photos – which we also describe in more detail from page 107.)

If the Photos app recognizes a person or group of people in a set of photos (based on the facial recognition you have done in the **People** albums – we get to that from page 45), it will include the collection of photos in the **Sharing Suggestions** section, with the option to share the collection with those named people.

'For You' -
Curated Collections of Photos

Other groups of photos may also appear in this **Sharing Suggestions** area – without any people suggested.

Swipe from right to left to view the suggestions for sharing.

Tap on any of the suggestions, then choose Next to see the list of suggested recipients (and to **Add People** if needed), then **Share in Messages** to send a link to a specially created temporary album in iCloud, one that will expire in 30 days.

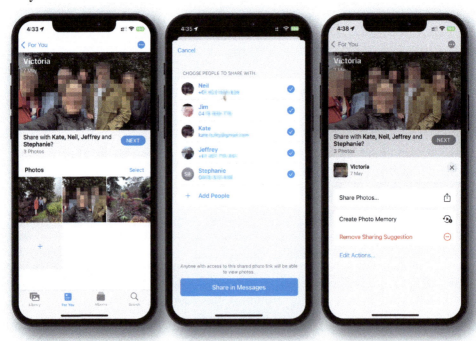

Or instead tap ••• at top right to see the option to **Share Photos**, which provides all the standard sharing options (Messages, Mail, Airdrop, etc).

Photos that you share in this way will appear in the **Recently Shared** area of **For You** – a section that will only appear if you have chosen to share any sets of photos in this way.

If you would like to remove any **Sharing Suggestion** item, tap ••• at top right of the selected suggestion, and choose **Remove Sharing Suggestion**. Or choose to **Create Photo Memory** if you want to keep that set as a Memory.

Where have you been?
The Places Album

The Places view of your photos Library shows your photos according to the location at which they were taken – for those photos that have location information stored in their metadata.

Along the top of this view, you will see two options – **Map** and **Grid** – providing different ways of viewing the groupings of your photos by 'place'.

In **Map** view, thumbnails of photos are shown on a map, where each thumbnail shows the number of photos taken at each location. Tap on any of these thumbnails to view those photos.

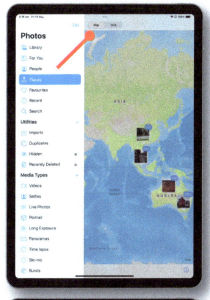

Use two fingers (spread them outwards or inwards) to Zoom in and out on this map to 'split out' your photos by their location.

Grid view shows the photos of places as thumbnails, grouped by location, for the area of the map that was in view.

View an individual photo by tapping on it.

Or tap the > next to the location associated with each group of photos to view the location's photos in something called **Explore View** (which provides a 'gallery style' view, from which you can play a

slideshow, view all the photos and more).

Tap the ⓘ at the bottom right of the Map view to see the different options for how to

Where have you been?
The Places Album

view the Map – Map, Hybrid (leftmost image below), Satellite (middle imge below) and 3D (rightmost image below.

This is an amazing feature, allowing you to revisit the places where your photos were taken.

If you don't see location recorded for the photos you take with the Camera app, this is because of a setting that has not been enabled.

Go to the Settings app – to **Settings -> Privacy and Security -> Location Services -> Camera**.

Select **While Using the App** and turn on **Precise Location** if you want to record the exact location. For privacy you may want to turn this off, in case you share any photos.

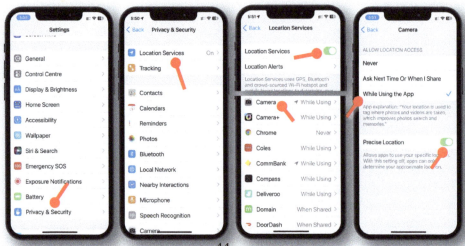

Organising your Photos - Find your People

Viewing your People

The **People** album (found in the top section of the left sidebar on iPad, and under the Album option on the iPhone) offers a great way of viewing all the photos of a particular person, using facial recognition to discover and group photos. The grouping of photos for the same person occurs automatically, but you can also manage this on a photo-by-photo basis. And you can merge separate groupings of photos that are of the same person.

The first time you visit the People album, your Photos app will show a set of thumbnails that represent groups of photos that have been determined as showing the same person. Tap on any of these thumbnails to view the set of photos that have been found for that person.

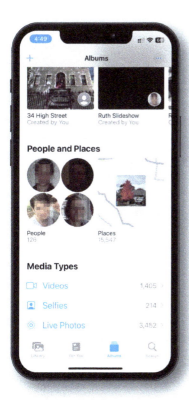 

45

Organising your Photos - Find your People

Name your people

As you can see in the iPad image on the previous page, several of the people thumbnails have names – but several others do not. To name any that are un-named, simply tap on the thumbnail and tap **Add Name** at the top and start typing the name of the person.

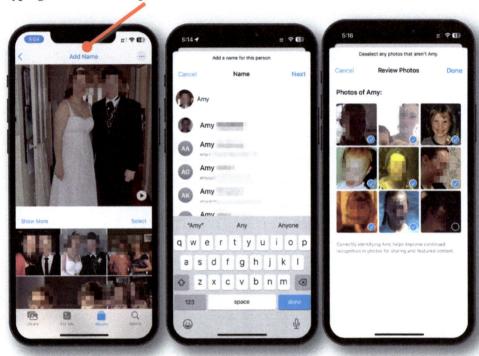

A list of suggested contacts will appear below (see middle image above). Tap on the relevant person, or (if the person is not a Contact) keep typing the name and choose enter/return to complete.

At that point, you may see another screen appear, asking for confirmation of some other faces that are deemed to be close matches to the person in the thumbnail that you just named.

Unselect (by tapping) those thumbnails that are not the same person as that you named, and then choose **Done**.

This will collate even more photos of that same person.

Organising your Photos - Find your People

If you name the person in the thumbnail and it is found that there is already a named thumbnail for that same person, the photos for that person will be merged.

View the photos for a person

For each identified person, tap the thumbnail to view the 'already-matched' photos of that person, shown as a 'Memories' style screen, with lots of ways of viewing photos of the person.

The top larger thumbnail is a slideshow of a selection of photos in the person's album.

Tap **Show More** to see all the match photos as thumbnails.

Tap on any thumbnail to view the individual photo, and swipe left to right (or right to left) to move through the photos.

You will also see the option to **Select** thumbnails, in which case options will appear along the bottom - to share, **Show Faces**, delete (bin) and 'more options' (circle with dots).

Show Faces is a handy option that allows you to view thumbnails that just show the person's face, so that you can more easily see if there are any incorrect matches. When in this mode, tap **Show Photos** to return to the normal view.

Remove unwanted People

You will probably see the faces of people you barely know or are not really important to you. These faces can be removed from the People album.

Organising your Photos - Find your People

This can be done from the thumbnail view by choosing Select at top right, then tapping to select the faces you don't want to see in the People album

Tap the **Remove** option at bottom left.

Confirm by selecting **Remove from People Album** when you see the confirmation message appear.

An alternative method of removing the person is to tap on their thumbnail (to view all the photos of that person), then choose ••• at top right and tap the **Remove This Person from People** option (for un-named people) or **Remove *person-name* from People** (if the person has been named) – see image below right.

Nominate your favourites

You will see the option to Favourite the selected people in the image directly above.

Your Favourite people appear at the top of the list of People thumbnails, in a separate section that has larger thumbnails than the rest.

Both screens shown on this page provide the option to **Favourite** the selected person.

The option to **Add *person-name* to Favourites** is found by on a thumbnail (to view all photos of that person), then choosing •••

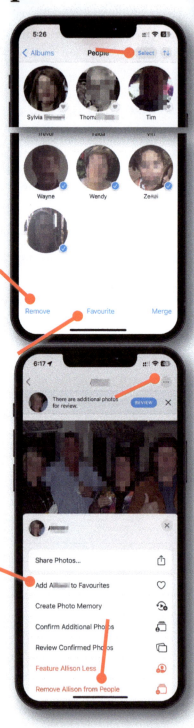

Organising your Photos - Find your People

Identifying more photos of the same person

For each identified person, tap the thumbnail view the 'already-matched' photos of that person, shown as a 'Memories' style screen with lots of ways of viewing photos of the person.

You may see a message at the top of this view – advising that there are additional photos that could be of the same person.

This will bring up the screen that we look at a couple of pages ago, for confirming whether other groups of photos are of the same person.

Untick any thumbnails that aren't of that person, then choose **Done**.

To look for further photos of that person, tap at ⋯ top right.

Tap **Confirm Additional Photos** to look for more photos of the same person.

Tap **Yes** if the photos IS of the person, and **No** otherwise.

Choose **Done** in the top bar to finish, or wait until you have exhausted all the possible potential matches.

You will notice that the matches get less accurate as you progress through the suggestions, often picking up other family members as likely matches.

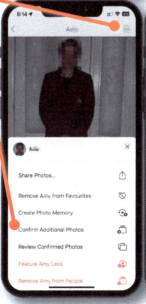

Organising your Photos - Find your People

When you finish this matching, the total number of additional photos that you just added for that person will show. Tap **Done** to finish the process.

Confirming just a few additional matches can add a substantial number of photos to the set collated for that person.

In the example here, 184 photos were added to this person's People album.

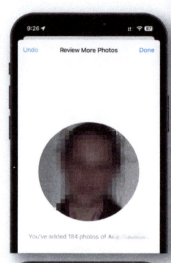

Merge People

If you see more than one thumbnail for the same person, the sets of photos represented by these thumbnails can be merged.

Choose **Select** at top right

Then tap to tick the two (or more) thumbnails that represent the person. Tap **Merge** in the bottom bar to merge the selected People albums.

To complete the merging, tap **Yes** when the confirmation appears.

As we have already covered, naming a previously un-named thumbnail with the same name as an already named thumbnail will also perform a Merge.

Organising your Photos -
Find your People

Identifying people while viewing photos

There is another way of updating your People album and adding to the photos for each of your people.

While you are viewing an individual photo, tap the ⓘ in the bottom bar (iPhone) or top bar (iPad).

If there are faces in the picture, small profile circles will appear at bottom left of the image.

If that circle has a blue question-mark on it, the person has not yet been identified as one of your People.

Tap on this and choose **Tag with Name**.

If that name is already an identified person in People, this photo and others that have been determined are the same person will be merged with that existing People album.

If the circles don't show a question-mark, then those people in the photo have already been identified.

Tap on the circle to see the options – as shown on right.

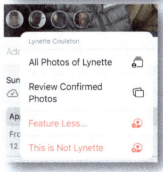

The name of the person will appear, with options to view the People album for the person, review the sets of photos that have been identified as that person, feature that person less in For You, and correct an incorrectly named person.

Organising your Photos - Find your People

When the wrong person appears in a People album

Of course, the face recognition technology is not perfect – so you may find that, when you have a look at the set of photos for a person, there are photos of other people included.

When you are look at the photo thumbnails in a People album, touch and hold on any photo to see a set of options – including **This is not person-name**. Tap this option remove the photo from that person's album.

Or tap **Select** at top right of the thumbnail view and tap to tick/select the photos that are not the person.

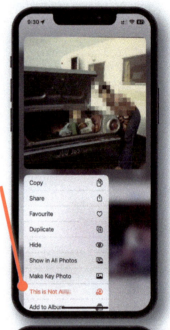

Then tap ⊙ at bottom right and tap **These are Not** *person-name*.

When viewing an individual photo from the People album, use the technique described in the previous section to remove the photo from that People album.

Another handy way of identifying a whole group of photos that have been incorrectly identifed as the person is to **Review Confirmed Photos**.

Tap the applicable person in the People view to see their album. Then tap ⊙ at top right to see this option.

This will provide a set of thumbnails that represent groups of photos identified as the same person, that that have been confirmed as collectively being of the person whose People album is being viewed.

Organising your Photos - Find your People

Scan through these and untick any that are not of the person, then choose **Done**.

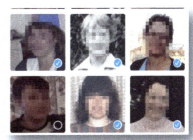

You will also notice in that option that there is the **Review More Photos** option at the bottom, if you are interested a that point in finding further photos of the person.

Make Key Photos

To change the photo that is used as the main 'thumbnail' for a person in the screen showing your collection of People, touch and hold on that preferred photo and choose **Make Key Photo**.

Sort People by Name (new in iOS/iPadOS 16)

When you build up a large set of People, it can be hard to find someone you are looking for.

The good news is that you can now sort the People album in alphabetical name order – making this much easier.

Tap the arrow symbols at top right of the People view. Choose either **Name** to sort in name order, or **Custom Order** to manually order the people thumbnails.

For Custom Order, touch and hold on any thumbnail and drag to a new location to manually rearrange.

Selecting Photos

We have already discussed in earlier sections the process of Selecting photos. But we include it her as its own section for easy reference.

Quite often, you will have the need to select more than one photo – for example, to select a set of photos to add to an album, to delete, to share and more. Let's look at how to do this. First though, you must always be in a view that shows full photo thumbnails.

1. Choose **Select** (top right).

2. Tap to select the photo/s you want to delete. Or drag your finger gently across the photos and downwards to select a large number quickly. You will see 'ticks' to show which photos you have selected.

3. Unselect any selected photos by tapping them (or dragging across the selected photos) to 'untick'.

4. Having selected a set of photos, you can then choose what to do with them – Share, Delete, or a range of other options available by tapping ⊙ at bottom right.

You will see options for adjusting Metadata for the set of photos, to **Add to Album** (new or existing – which we'll cover shortly), Favourite them and more.

Refer back to this section whenever we talk about selecting multiple photos.

Deleting photos

Understanding 'Delete' vs 'Remove'

Photos can be **Deleted** individually, or as part of a selection. Just tap the Trash Can to delete any photo.

But before we discuss the deletion methods, we need to first discuss the difference between '**Removing**' and '**Deleting**' a photo.

Always make sure you check the message that appears when you are deleting, to confirm if you are actually 'deleting' or 'removing'. What do I mean by this?

If you are looking at photos in one of the standard albums or in the Library area (via Days, All Photos, People, Places, Recent, Videos, Selfies etc.) and you choose to Delete any of these photos, you will be choosing to delete them from photos library.

The deleted photos will go into the **Recently Deleted** album and be permanently deleted after 30 days (approximately) - unless you specifically choose to remove them sooner.

If you have iCloud Photos enabled, you will (after 30 days) be permanently deleting them from iCloud and all other devices that use that same iCloud Photos library.

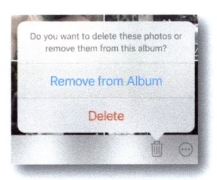

If you are looking at a set of photos that are in an Album that <u>you have created</u> (we'll look at creating your own albums shortly), you can choose to just Remove from Album, but leave them on your device (and in iCloud Photos, if applicable), and in any other Album that you have added them to.

(That is, unless you specifically choose the Delete option from the confirmation message.)

Deleting Photos

Deleting a single photo/video

1. Tap on the photo's thumbnail to view that photo.

2. If you only see the photo and no options, tap on the screen to see your bar/s of options at the top and bottom.

3. To delete, choose the Trash Can at bottom right (on the iPhone) or the top right (on the iPad).

4. Tap **Delete** or **Remove** in the confirmation message to complete the function – and make sure you read it to check whether you are removing or deleting.

Deleting/Removing several photos

1. Use the method described earlier to select several photos/videos.

2. You will also see that the footer changes to show the number of photos that you have selected, and that the 'trash can' appears at bottom right.

3. Tap on the Trash Can to delete or the selected photo/s.

4. Tap **Remove from Album** or **Delete** in the confirmation message to complete the deletion (or removal) of the photos.

Deleting Photos

Some hidden space gobblers to delete

The Camera app provides the capability to take 'Bursts' of photos - rapid-fire photos taken by holding down the white dot on older iPhones and iPads, or by sliding the white dot to the left on newer iPhones. If you use this feature (either deliberately or accidentally), you may find yourself with quite a few 'bursts' of several photos, instead of just the single photo that you want.

Visit the **Bursts** album under Media Types (in Albums on iPhone, in the Sidebar of the iPad – which only appears if there are Bursts of photos) to find and eradicate the excess photos.

In the example shown here, I can see that there are several sets of 'bursts' in my **Bursts** album.

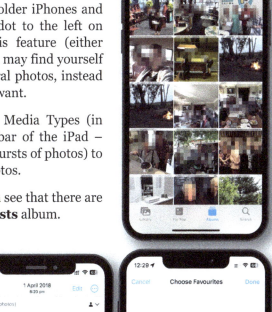

What I really want to do is choose the best of each set of photos and delete the rest.

To do this, tap a photo thumbnail to view one of the 'bursts' (see image on right).

At the top left, you will see the number of photos that are in the 'Burst' (in the example on the right, there are 5).

Look for Select ....

This will be at the bottom on the iPhone, and the top left on the iPad.

Deleting Photos

This provides a mode where you can select which photo/s of the 'Burst' that you want to keep.

Along the bottom is a ribbon of the photos in the burst.

Drag this ribbon from left to right (and right to left) see each of the photos in the 'Burst'. Tap to tick the best photo (or several photos if you want to keep more than one).

Once you have chosen which photos you want to keep from the burst, choose **Done** at top right.

If you have only elected to keep one (or some) of the burst's photos, you will be asked what to do with those that you didn't select.

Usually, you will want to tap **Keep Only n Favourites**, so that the unselected photos are moved to the **Recently Deleted** album (and eventually deleted).

Organising Photos into your own Albums

You can really make your iPad (or iPhone) into a beautiful digital photo album by arranging your photos into your own Albums.

This is a great way of showcasing your photos to family and friends, and a great way of organising your images so that you can find them when you need them!

As previously described, the Albums that you create are found under **My Albums**. On the iPad, My Albums is found as a section in the left sidebar. On the iPhone, it is found at the top of the **Albums** view (by tapping the **Albums** option in the bottom bar).

There are two ways to create albums:

1. Create the album, then add photos to it or

2. Select a group of photos, then choose to create a new album (or add to an existing album)

We'll look at each of these methods. (Note. I always use Method 2 as I find it much easier.)

Method 1: Create an album, then add the photos

To create the album, you must first be viewing the All Albums area on the iPad or be viewing the main Albums view on the iPad (as shown below). Look for the + symbol, which shows at the top left of the Albums view on the iPhone and at the top left of the main area on the iPad.

Organising Photos
into your own Albums

Note that if you were already viewing an individual album within this area, you will not see this + symbol. On the iPhone, tap < at top left to get back to the 'top' level of the Albums area. On the iPad, tap **All Albums** in the sidebar.

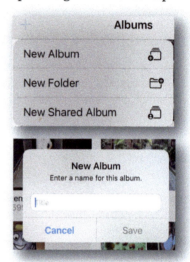

The + option will provide a menu of 3 options on the iPhone as shown below. On the iPad, you will only see the top two option.

To create a new Album, choose **New Album**, then provide a name for your new Album and tap **Save**.

You will then have the option to choose one or more photos to add to this new album. Tap to select photos, then choose **Add** at top right.

Your new album will then appear alongside the **Recent** and **Favourites** albums.

Method 2: Select some photos, then create the album

This is my preferred method – to select some photos, and then create the album – or perhaps add them to an existing album.

Use the method that is described on page 54 to select a set of photos.

Tap ⊙ at bottom right or ⬆ at bottom left. Both provide the **Add to Album** option.

Organising Photos into your own Albums

You will then have the option to select **New Album** (and name your new album, same as described above), or to tap to choose an existing Album from the list shown under the heading **My Albums**.

We will talk shortly about Folders, which are groupings of Albums (and perhaps other folders).

Note that photos can only be added to Albums, not Folders.

Adding Photos to an Album

The easiest way to add photos to an Album in My Albums is to follow the steps just described, to select a set of photos and then choose Tap at bottom right, then tap ⊙ or ⛉ and the **Add to Album** option – and choose the applicable existing Album.

Syncing of Albums between devices

If you <u>haven't</u> turned on iCloud Photos (described later from page 107), Albums created on your iPad or iPhone aren't synced to your computer and to other Apple mobile Devices.

When you import your photos to your computer (by plugging the device into the computer with a USB cable) the Albums you created aren't imported with them.

So if you want to see the same set of Albums across all your devices, you will need to use iCloud Photos.

Photos are not Moved to Albums

It is important to note again that, as mentioned earlier, photos are not moved into albums when you choose to add the photo to an album.

Albums are effectively an index into your Photos library – a list of photo IDs and where to find them in the Library, that is used to display a group of photos together.

Photos are stored once only (unless you specifically duplicate them).

Organising Photos into your own Albums

So don't fall into the trap of thinking that you have 'moved' them to an Album can therefore delete them from other views.

If you choose **Delete**, you will be deleting from the entire library, including any Album you have created. And, if you use iCloud, you will also be deleting from iCloud and all other devices that are connected to that same iCloud Account.

The below image attempts to provide a visual representation of this concept, showing the main Photos Library view, then the My Albums that have been created to show certain photos from that library – where a photo can appear in multiple My Albums.

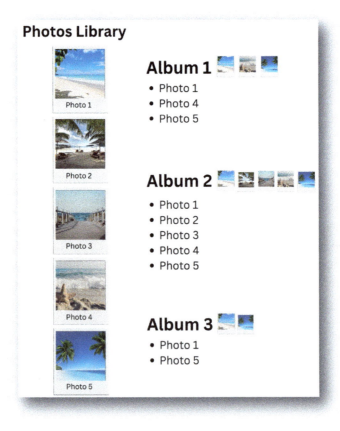

Organising Photos into your own Albums

Renaming an Album

If you want to rename an album on your iPad or iPhone, touch and hold on the Album's thumbnail and choose **Rename Album**. Make the necessary changes to the name and choose Save. On the iPad you can also touch and hold on the Album name in the left sidebar.

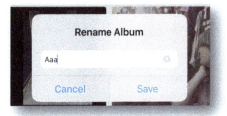

Alternatively, there is the Edit option that appears at top right when you are viewing all your albums.

To see your full set of My Albums, tap See All in Albums view on the iPhone and **All Albums** in the iPad's sidebar.

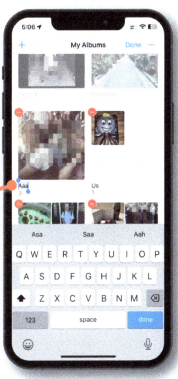

When in **Edit** mode, tap on any Album name to see the keyboard pop up and the name highlighted, ready to be replaced or change.

Once you have changed the Album name/s, select Done top right to exit **Edit** mode.

Organising Photos
into your own Albums

Re-Arranging Albums

While your Albums view is in Edit mode (as described on the previous page), hold your finger on an Album's thumbnail for about a second – it will magnify a bit.

<u>Without lifting your finger</u>, drag that thumbnail to the required position and let go.

Repeat for any other albums you want to move.

Touch **Done** (top right) when finished in **Edit** mode.

Deleting an album

While your Albums view is in **Edit** mode (as described on the previous page, tap ● at top left of the thumbnail. Then **Delete** to confirm.

As shown in the confirmation message above, the photos are not deleted when an Album is deleted.

The album contents will still be available in other views and any other albums that they have been added to.

Organise Albums using Folders

Albums can be further organised further into Folders. In fact, a whole folder/subfolder structure can be established.

Photos cannot be added directly to a Folder – they can only be added to Albums. Folders are simply a way of organizing/grouping your Albums.

In the example shown on right, the second thumbnail from the top has the name **Family**.

Tapping Family reveals that this folder has both Albums and Folders in it (see below).

Cakes and **30th Anniversary** are both Albums. **Christmas** is a Folder containing 3 Albums.

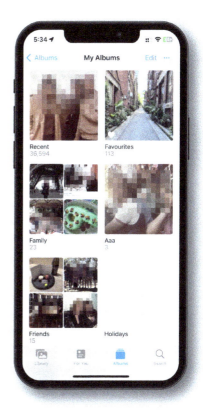

To create a top level Folder in My Albums, choose the + symbol at top left of the main **Albums** view on the iPhone, or in the All Albums view on the iPad, and choose **New Folder.**

Name your Folder, then choose Save.

Tap on the Folder thumbnail to open that folder.

To then add another Folder or an Album to that Folder, tap Edit at top right, then + at top left.

It is important to note that, on an iPhone or iPad, you can't add existing Albums to a Folder. You can only add new Albums to a Folder. This limitation does not exist on

Organise Albums using Folders

the Mac – so it is best to work with Folders there (if you use iCloud Photos) and the changes you make there will sync to your iPad and iPhone.

Renaming, rearranging and Deleting Folders works the same as already described for Albums.

We won't spend any further words on this one, as it is of limited value without that ability to add an existing Album to a Folder. We certainly hope that the next iOS and iPadOS upgrade includes the ability to add existing Albums to Folders.

Sharing Photos and Videos

You can share the photos on your iPad and iPhone in emails, text messages, via Airdrop or 'Shared Albums' (via iCloud), in Twitter posts, on Facebook and more.

Choose to share an individual photo or video, or several at once (limits apply in certain cases though).

Videos can be shared in email and text messages, and even on YouTube.

Sharing a single photo or video

To share anything from your iPad or iPhone, always look for the **Share** symbol.

When you have an individual photo or video in view, tap □ - at top left on the iPad and bottom left on the iPhone.

If you don't see the Share symbol, tap the screen to make the top and bottom bars appear again.

The **Share** menu allows you to choose from the list of options provided. Just touch on the required option.

We'll cover some of these next.

Sharing Photos and Videos

If you decide you don't want to proceed with the share right now, choose ⊗ at top right.

Send or share several photos.

If you wish to send several photos, use the selection method described earlier (see page 54) to select the required photos.

Then choose the symbol ⬆️ (found at bottom left of the selection screen) to see the options for sharing.

Alternatively, when you have already selected a single image to Share, the Share screen (see right) will allow you to swipe left and right through the images and tap to tick or untick further photos.

A count of the number selected is shown at the top.

Some Options before sending

Some special choices can be made for the photos that are selected, by tapping the word **Options** - which appears at the top of the Share screen.

Under **Send As** are options that allow the choice of how the photos will be shared - as attached photos/videos or an iCloud Link (which we'll talk about next) or allowing the Photos app to work this out based on the total file size of the content you are sharing.

The **Automatic** option only applies to sharing via Messages.

Note that these **Send As** options will only appear if you have chosen to use iCloud Photos – described further on page 107.

Also available is the option to choose whether you wish to share any location information from the photos/videos, and whether you want to share all other metadata associated with the photo/s – which will send the original along with any edits you have applied.

Sharing Photos and Videos

Share using an iCloud Link

If you have enabled iCloud Photos (which is covered from page 107), there is a great option of using iCloud to share a set of photos – by creating and sending just an iCloud Link to the recipient.

We have already seen on the previous page that such a link can be created by choosing **Options** at the top of the Share screen (see below right) and choosing **iCloud Link** (see image on right).

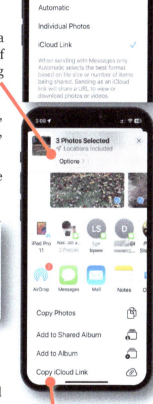

When you choose Done after selecting **iCloud Link**, your photos will be uploaded to iCloud, to a special, temporary web page that will only exist for 30 days.

The link to this temporary web page will then be copied to your device's Clipboard[1].

Depending on how many photos/videos you have selected for the iCloud Link, you may see the message on the right.

If you have chosen several photos or there are videos included, this message could take a little while to go away – so be patient.

Having created the iCloud Link, tap Messages or Mail (or any other email app that you wish to use), and the just-created link will appear in the draft message or email.

To simply create such an iCloud Link that you can then choose to paste elsewhere, **Select** the photos to be shared, then choose the **Copy iCloud Link**

---

[1] The **Clipboard** is an area in the device's memory where copied content goes, content that you intend to 'paste' elsewhere. Each 'copy' that is performed replaces the previous content of the Clipboard. After pasting, the content usually remains in the Clipboard until replaced by a further copy, or until the device re-starts.

Sharing Photos and Videos

option from the list of options that appear below the app symbols.

This will copy the iCloud Link to the clipboard and exit the Share menu.

Then, open your Mail app or your Messages app and paste the generated link into the body of the email or message.

When the recipient taps/clicks that link, they will be taken to a web page that shows the photos you have uploaded – and gives them the option to **Download** those photos into their own Photos library.

As mentioned, the generated iCloud Link will expire after 30 days, at which point its temporary web page will be deleted. (Your original photos will still remain in your Photos library.)

To see the iCloud Links that are currently active and to copy any link to the clipboard again, visit the **For You** option on your iPad (second option from top in iPad sidebar, and second option in bottom bar on iPhone).

You will see an **iCloud Links** section if any such links exist, with thumbnails representing each of the links and content.

Touch and hold on any thumbnail you see in the **iCloud Links** section to choose to **Copy iCloud Link** or to **Stop Sharing** – to delete the temporary web page associated with the link.

Sharing Photos and Videos

To see all the content that is shared using that iCloud Link, tap the thumbnail. You will also see the expiry date for the link.

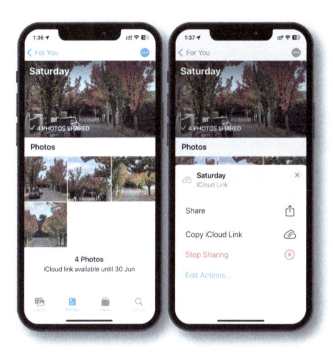

Tap 💬 at top right to see the options to **Share** the link again, to **Copy iCloud Link** to the clipboard again, and to **Stop Sharing** (if the link is no longer required).

Sharing Photos and Videos

Emailing photos

Choose the **Mail** option in the Share menu to send one or more photos/videos via email.

If you send multiple images in a mail message, just make sure that the email you are creating is not too big to send. All email providers have limits on the size of what can be sent.

As mentioned on page 69, you can choose (from Options) to send an iCloud Link there are lots to send and if the email will be too large.

For images being sent in the email, you can control the file size of these images, and send smaller versions than the originals.

Working out and controlling the file size of your email differs for the Mail app on the iPad and the iPhone.

On the iPad, if the email with images will be over 500KB, you will see the total size of the images in the email in the field **Images**.

Tap this word to see the options for **Image Size**, and the size that the email will be for each choice of image size.

Tap the size that you prefer – I tend to go with Medium or Small, unless the person needs higher resolution versions of the photos.

This image size setting will then be 'remembered' for the next email that you send via Mail.

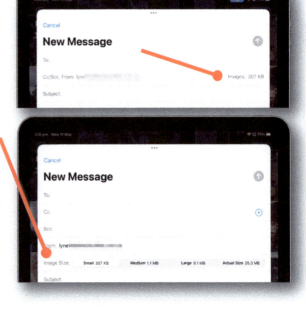

Sharing Photos and Videos

This means that, if you adjust the size to Medium when sending a set of photos via Mail today, then the next time you create an email in Mail with photos, they will be automatically sized as Medium.

This can then be changed if you require a different sizing next time around – and will again be 'remembered'.

For the iPhone, the size of the photos that you send in the email is not set until you hit **Send**.

The various size options appear, as shown on right.

Once again, choose the size that you require. Once you tap the size option, your message will send.

If you chose the iCloud Link option from Options before choosing Mail as your method of sharing, the email that is generated will look something like that below right.

A suggested subject/topic will describe the photos associated with the link, words that you can change.

Just don't change the link!

As is also shown in the email on the right, the message will include the expiry date for the iCloud Link.

Sending Photos/Videos via Messages

If you want to send your photos/videos as a Message, consider first whether the person you are sending them to is an iMessage user.

If they are not – i.e. your messages to them are sent as an SMS/Text Message (green in colour, using phone/text) instead of an internet message (using internet – over mobile on Wi-Fi connection) – consider sending more than one or two photos and any videos as an iCloud Link, to avoid MMS charges that might apply for both you and the recipient.

Sharing Photos and Videos

Even if they are an iMessage user, it can be a good idea to send a large number of photos – or a video – as an iCloud Link. In fact, your Share may choose to automatically generate a link if the Automatic option is applicable in Options (described on page 68).

Sent via iCloud Expires 7 Jul

Sending the photos as an iCloud Link will mean that a recipient with iMessage sees a preview of the photos, with **Send via iCloud** underneath, along with the expiry date of the link – as shown in the image on the right.

For recipients who are not iMessage users, the received message will be a text message and the link will look something like that shown in the image on right. They will need to have an internet connection to be able to view the photos/videos.

Sharing photos using Airdrop

AirDrop

If you are looking to share photos or videos with another Apple user who is nearby (i.e. a matter of metres away), Airdrop allows for such sharing without even requiring an internet connection – using Bluetooth instead.

Both Wi-Fi and Bluetooth must be turned ON if you would like to use Airdrop.

This can be very handy for a sharing a large group of photos or videos, avoiding size limits that may apply to email or messages and any other sharing method that requires internet access. It is also much quicker than sharing via the internet.

You (and those with whom you wish to share your photos) can choose whether the Airdrop feature is enabled from the **Control Centre**. From there, you choose who can Airdrop to you (Contacts Only, or Everyone).

Sharing Photos and Videos

(See more on how to enable and use Airdrop in the iTandCoffee book, **Introduction to the iPad and iPhone - A Guided Tour**.)

Airdrop is available in the row of app options in the Share menu. You may also see a suggested Airdrop device in the icons directly below the image thumbnails.

Tap the Airdrop option in the Share menu to see the full list of available nearby devices, then tap on the applicable recipient device and wait for the 'send' to complete.

The person receiving the photo/s or video/s must agree to accept the photos that you send.

When they accept on their iPad or iPhone, the received content will be added to their Photos library. It will be the most recent item/s in the Recent album.

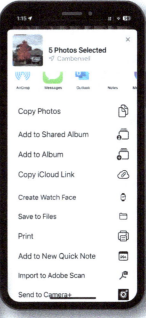

On the Mac, the recipient will have the option to **Accept** and then to **Save to Downloads** or to **Open in Photos** (see below).

Sharing an Album of Photos using iCloud

A set of photos can also be shared in alternative way using your iCloud, by setting up **Shared Albums** that can be shared with multiple people – even those who are not users of Apple devices.

We cover this in our look at iCloud Photos (Page 107).

Sharing Photos and Videos

Share the photo/s or video/s with another App

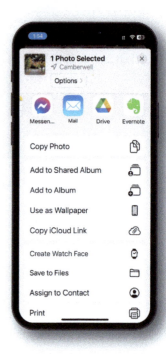

If you have installed certain apps on your device, those apps appear as options in your Share menu that appears in the Photos app.

Tapping on any of those options will, generally copy your photo to that app, for use in or by that app.

Assign photo to a Contact

If the photo is of a person, you will have the option assign the photo to the applicable person in your Contacts, by choose the **Assign to Contact** option.

Then, when they call you, the photo you have chosen will appear!

Print your photos

The **Share** screen provides the **Print** option in the bottom set of options.

If you have an **Airprint** capable printer (i.e. a Wi-Fi printer that is compatible with the iPad or iPhone), choose this option to print to that printer.

Use a photo as your Wallpaper

If you have a single photo selected when you choose Share, you can choose to **Use as Wallpaper.**

On the iPhone, this allows for the creation of a new Lock Screen/Wallpaper pair.

On the iPad, the image can be be used on either the Lock or Home Screen or both.

We won't go into the topic of Wallpapers further in this guide, as it is a topic covered in the book **Introduction to the iPad and iPhone – A Guided Tour**.

Viewing your photos as a Slideshow

The Slideshow option will automatically cycle through an album, a selection of photos, or perhaps even all your photos. You can have fancy 'transitions', and you can put your show to music.

The **Slideshow** option is available when you are viewing thumbnails of photos in an Album – or perhaps have just **Select**ed a set of photos.

Tap ⬤ and choose **Slideshow**.

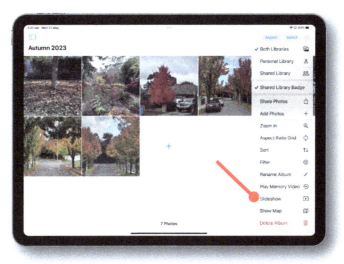

The slideshow will start immediately, perhaps with music.

Viewing your photos as a Slideshow

When the top and bottom bars are visible (tap the screen if you don't see these), you will be given some **Options** for customizing your slideshow (see second image on previous page).

Tap **Options** at bottom right, and choose:

- **Theme** – the style of the slideshow and transitions between photos.

- **Music** – choose from the standard range based on theme or use your own music from the Music Library (must be purchased or imported – can't be Apple Music content). Tap **Music Library** to make your choice.

- Whether you want the slideshow to play over and over – slide the **Repeat** option to On (green).

- **The speed** of the slideshow – slide towards the turtle to see photos for longer, or towards the hare for quicker transitions between photos.

Play Memory Video

A relatively new option is to choose to **Play Memory Video** for the album's photos.

This allows for the creation of a video like those shown in Memories in the **For You** area.

And you can save your Memory Video as a Favourite to that area, so that you can re-play it easily later.

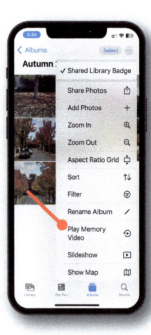

Viewing your photos as a Slideshow

Tap ⊞ at bottom right to see the photos and perhaps remove one or more from the memory video. Tap ••• at top right to see the options for the Memory Video – to **Select** photos to remove, to add as a Favourite Memory, to edit the name.

Tap 🎵 to select the music mix for your Memory Video. The music

Swipe right-to-left (and vice-versa) to peruse the suggested Mixes (some with filters).

Tap from that view to choose a Filter 🔘 (or Memory Look) – see image on right.

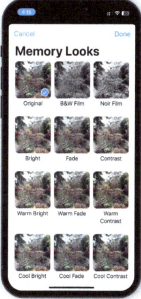

And tap 🎵 to choose your own music – which can be from the full Apple Music library in this case.

Hopefully that gives enough of an overview of this feature - we'll leave you to explore it further on your own.

Editing your Photos

What sort of Editing is possible?

Quite often, the photos that we take can be made so much better with some
minor (or major!) adjustments. Lots of editing capabilities are provided by the
Photos app on your iPad and iPhone, including:

- Enhance
- Crop
- Rotate

- Aspect Ratio
- Red-Eye
- Filters

- Adjust
- Extensions

We will look at each of these editing features in turn shortly.

How do I get to these editing options?

When you are viewing **an individual photo**, you will see the Edit option at
the top right of the screen.

If, when viewing an individual photo, you don't see the **Edit** option (or, in fact,
any other options), just tap on the screen to reveal the bars at the top and
bottom. Tapping **Edit** will reveal a range of options on either side and at top
(on iPad) and at top and bottom (on iPhone)

Editing your Photos

Just tap on any of the **Edit** options/symbols to make the necessary changes to your Photo. You can apply as many as you like and choose Done at top right (iPad) or bottom right (iPhone) when you are finished.

Your original photo is retained

It is important to note that edits applied to your photo are cumulative, but do not replace the original photo.

At any point, you can revert to the original version of the photo or video – or choose to duplicate the edited photo/video and revert one of the versions to the original while keeping the edits in the other.

To see the original version of the photo at any time, just tap on the image while in **Edit** mode. You will briefly see the original, before returning to the edited version – allowing for a comparison of the two versions.

Undoing edits

If the photo has been previously edited, the Revert option will appear at bottom right (iPhone), or top right (iPad).

If you apply any edits, the Done option will appear, allowing you to finish editing, while **Cancel** will exit Edit mode without applying the edits you may just have made.

As you apply edits, you will notice that the arrow symbols at top right become available. The back-arrow **undoes** the edit you just applied, and the forward-arrow **re-applies** the edit you just undid.

Enhance

Enhance can provide a quick-fix for a not-so-great photo.

It balances the darks and lights and improves the contrast and brightness. Just touch on the **Enhance** 'wand' to see what a difference it makes. The wand icon will have a light-grey background if the enhance has already been applied.

If you touch **Enhance** again, the auto-enhance feature will turn off and your image will return to its un-enhanced state.

Editing your Photos

Crop

The **Crop** feature of Edit mode allows you the change the borders of the photo – to cut out part of the photo or zoom in on the main area of interest. It also includes lots of other adjustments – to straighten, adjust perspective, and set the 'aspect ratio'. Let's take a look at these.

Crop the photo

In **Crop** mode, you will see a border appear around your image with 'tabs' at each corner and in the middle of each side.

To crop the photo, simply drag the corners in and out, up and down. Or drag top down, bottom up, or sides inwards.

Drag the photo around within the new framed area to adjust the positioning of the features of the photo within the frame.

Pinch inwards and outwards to zoom in and out within the frame.

At any point, the **Crop** changes you have made can be undone using the **RESET** option at the top.

To complete any cropping you have applied, choose **Done**.

Straighten your image

The Crop option allows for the straightening of your photo using the graded line at the bottom.

If you see the **AUTO** option at the top, tap this to automatically straighten your photo.

Or, drag the graded line (also called 'the slider') left and right (on iPhone) or up and down (on iPad) to see the angle of the photo change.

Editing your Photos

When adjusting the angle of the photo, there are three options – a plain 'straighten' option (leftmost icon in image on right), as well as vertical and horizontal perspective adjustments (middle and right icons respectively). Tap on the required option, then drag the line to see the adjustments.

Have a play with these to see the effects. You can always tap **Cancel** to undo what you have just done.

Set the Aspect Ratio

The Crop option allows for the **Aspect Ratio** of the photo to be changed, which then controls the cropping.

Aspect Ratio refers to the width and height proportions for the image.

Tap the symbol at top right when in crop mode) to choose from **Original, Freeform, Square, Wallpaper, 2:3, 3:5, 3:4, 4:5, 5:7 and 9:16.**

More recent versions of iOS/iPadOS have seen the addition of the options **Freeform** (which is the default) and **Wallpaper** (iPhone only).

For all except Freeform, tap the required Aspect Ratio to 'lock' the proportions so that, when you 'crop' the photo, it maintains these proportions.

Rotate your photo

Also in Crop mode is the option for rotating your photo. Touch on the **Rotate** option to rotate the image 90° anti-clockwise. Keep tapping **Rotate** until your image is oriented correctly.

Flip Horizontal

If the photo is 'back to front', tap the 'flip horizontal' symbol in Crop mode to flip it.

Editing your Photos

Filters

Filters provides a way of changing the colours and tones of your image with a number of special effects, such as black and white, faded, a 'polaroid' look, and a few others.

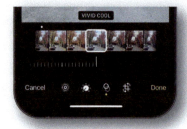

Tap the filter symbol (bottom on iPhone), left on iPad) to see the options and drag the bar of options to view each. Choose the leftmost (iPhone) or top (iPad) option - **Original** - to remove any filter that you have applied.

Red Eye

We've all seen those photos taken with a flash, where the person in the shot looks like they are possessed – with red eye/s.

Your iPad and iPhone allow you to remove red eyes from photos really easily.

Just touch on **Red Eye** symbol at the top of the Edit screen if it is visible. It will only appear if red eye is detected.

You will see an instruction along the bottom: **Tap each red eye.**

Editing your Photos

Just touch on a red eye in your photo.

You will see the red in the eye change to black.

If you are unhappy, tap the eye again to remove the correction and try again.

If necessary, you can 'zoom in' by using the 'pinch outwards' gesture.

Repeat this for each red eye in the shot, then touch the **Done** option to finish editing (or continue with further edits).

Adjust

Tapping on the Adjust option gives a range of options to adjust lighting, colour, and so much more.

- Exposure
- Brilliance
- Highlights
- Shadows
- Contrast
- Adjust
- Black Point
- Saturation
- Vibrance
- Warmth
- Tint
- Sharpness
- Definition
- Noise Reduction
- Vignette

For each of these options, you will see a slider that can be dragged back and forth (or up and down on iPad) to adjust that setting.

I'll leave those of you who are more advanced photo editors to have a play with these options.

If you ever want to 'back out' of your changes, just tap **Cancel**.

A HANDY TIP

To compare the adjusted photo with the unadjusted version, tap on the photo while in Edit mode to see the pre-edit version.

Editing your Photos

Markup

Markup is a very handy option that allows you to 'draw on' an image, add a text box, and perform various other 'markup' operations.

Tap the pencil to see the various markup options along the bottom. Tap + for additional options.

We won't cover this in detail here, but it is worth checking out and having a play with.

Extensions

The Extensions option allows you to access Photo editing features from other apps that you have on your iPad or iPhone.

Note that only some photo editing apps (not all) offer such extensions, allowing them to be used from the Photos app.

To see if you have any such apps, tap on the Extensions icon at top right.

Tap on any app you see there to use that app's Extension features, then **Done** at top right to to go back to the main **Edit** option of Photos.

My favourite extensions are from an app called **Camera +**, which provides some really great 'auto-enhance' features. (This app is not free.)

Skitch is a free app from the makers of Evernote, allowing you to quickly add arrows, boxes, text, pixelate part of the image and more. I use this one very regularly on the iPad, iPhone and my Mac.

86

Editing your Photos

Live Photo Edits

If your photo was taken with the Live feature (which is described further on page 35), then you will see the 'live' symbol (as shown above) in the bottom bar of options on the iPhone and on the left of side on the iPad.

If the photo is <u>not</u> a Live photo, no such symbol will appear in Edit mode.

Tap this symbol, and at the top of the screen you will see a yellow box if the Live feature is enabled for the photo, and no colour if the Live feature is disabled.

Tap this box to turn the Live feature on or off.

If it is off, the photo becomes a still photo and no short video will play when you touch and hold on the photo.

A Live photo may also have some audio associated with it, and this audio can be disabled from Edit mode.

Tap the speaker symbol at top left to turn off (or on) the recorded audio. Yellow means it is on, grey means it is off.

When the Live feature is enabled, you will notice a strip of photos at the bottom when viewing the Live edit features.

This strip allows you to choose the **Key Photo** that is shown for the Live photo – i.e. the photo that appears in the Photos, Memories and Albums.

Tap on each little thumbnail until your find the photo that you want to use as this Key Photo, then tap **Make Key Photo**.

You will often find a better version than what has been automatically chosen as that key photo.

Editing your Photos

Portrait Photo Edits

iPhones since the iPhone 7 – and some iPads – can take a type a photo called a **Portrait** photo – a photo that uses something called **Depth Effect**, to blur the background and focus on the object in the foreground.

Such a photo will show ⊘ PORTRAIT at the top when viewing the photo, and when in **Edit** mode.

In edit mode, you can turn **Portrait Mode** on and off simply by tapping the word **Portrait.** This will remove the ⊘PORTRAIT blurring effect.

Tap ⊘PORTRAIT to restore the effect.

At top left are two symbols.

The left symbol represents Lighting Effects; the right represents the 'depth' of the focus and blurring.

Let's take a look at these portrait photo editing features.

Portrait Photos – Lighting Effects ⬡

Different lighting effects can be applied to the Portrait photo using the set of options shown underneath the Portrait photo in the **Edit** screen.

If you don't see these symbols, tap ⬡ at top left to show this Lighting Effects bar.

The symbol will change to ⬡ , and the lighting effect options will appear under the phot.

Tap any of the symbols to see and choose from the different lighting effect options.

Editing your Photos

Examples of these lighting effects are shown below – Natural light, Studio light, Contour light, Stage light, Stage light Mono and High-key light mono.

Editing your Photos

Portrait Photos – Depth

Tap the depth symbol at top left to adjust the level of blurring and focus. A slider will appear. Dragging to the leftmost position will give the maximum blur, while the rightmost position will give no blur.

Tapping the Lighting Effects symbol again will show the depth symbol with the applicable depth level.

Copying edits to other photos

A feature that arrived in iOS/iPadOS 16 is the ability to copy edits that have been applied to one photo across to other photos.

To copy the edits that have been applied to a photo, tap then tap **Copy Edits**.

This option is also available from Edit mode, by tapping the same symbol.

Then, **Select** the photo or photos to which you want to apply the same edits, then choose the same symbol again.

You will see the option to **Paste Edits**. Tap this to apply the same edits to the selected photos.

Another way to Revert to Original

You will also notice that the menu offers the **Revert to Original** option for any photo or video that has been Edited.

Editing Videos

Just like for photos, other Editing options are also available for your videos – to crop, apply a filter, adjust and more. But let's talk about some editing that is specific to videos.

Trim Video

The videos in Photos can be very easily trimmed, to remove unneeded footage from the start or end.

Select the video you wish to edit and choose Edit.

Along the bottom, you will see a bar, with arrows at either end.

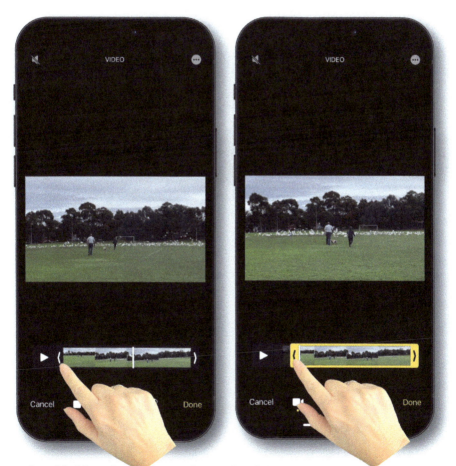

Touch and hold on the arrow at either end and drag it to change where the video should start or end. You will see the bar outline and background of the arrows turn yellow.

Editing Videos

While the strip appears like this, drag the left edge of the bar to the right and/or the right edge of the bar to the left to trim the start and end.

Select **Done** when you have finished your trimming.

You will then be asked to choose whether to save the trimmed video as a new video - **Save as New Clip** – or replace the longer video – **Save Video** - to replace the longer version.

 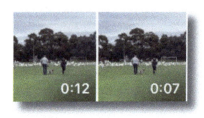

Where is my trimmed video?

If you choose to **Save Video as New Clip**, the untrimmed and trimmed video will appear alongside each other in the **Videos** album, and in the **All Photos** view (in the Library timeline).

If you go looking for your trimmed video in your **Recent** album, you will find that the new video is not next to the original. It will instead be the last item in your Recent album.

This is because the Recent album show photos and videos in the order that they were added to your iPad or iPhone, not in the 'date taken' order.

Turn off Audio in Video

Your video will probably have some audio associated with it.

If don't want this audio to play when you watch the video, turn it off from Edit mode.

Tap 🔊 to change it to 🔇 and choose **Done** at bottom right. Your video will be saved without the Audio.

Duplicating Photos and Videos

On occasion, it may be necessary the take a copy of a photo or video – perhaps before you apply some edits, so that you can keep both the edited and unedited versions of the photo side by side. As mentioned earlier, this can also be done after editing – and edits removed from one of the versions.

First, select one or more photos using the selection method described earlier in the guide.

Look for the  symbol – which will be at top right if are viewing an individual photo, and at bottom right if you have selected several photos.

Tap the **Duplicate** option that appears in the list of options.

When looking at the **All Photos** option in in the Library view, the duplicated photo/s or video/s will be found alongside the original/s.

In the **Recent** album, the duplicate/s will be the last item/s.

If you have applied any edits to the duplicated photo, you can then edit one of the versions and choose to **Revert** – so that you have both the original and edied versions of the same photo.

Searching for Photos

The **Search** feature allows for searching for photos/videos based on a wide range of search criteria, such as

- Place
- Person/Face
- Date or Date range, or maybe a month, or year
- Category/object - e.g. Christmas Tree, Tree, Water, Dog, Cat
- Caption text

The Search option is in the bottom bar, rightmost option on the iPhone and in the sidebar on the iPad. If you don't see it, you are probably viewing an individual photo – so return to the level above to see this option.

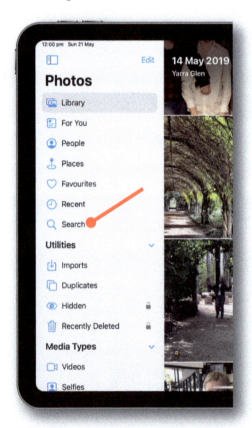 

A search bar appears at the top, as well as some suggestions for sets of photos below that.

For example, if I tap the Autumn thumbnail, I will see a set of photos that have been identified as having been taken in Autumn.

Searching for Photos

There are sections for People, Place, Category and Group suggestions, plus a list of recent search phrases you have used.

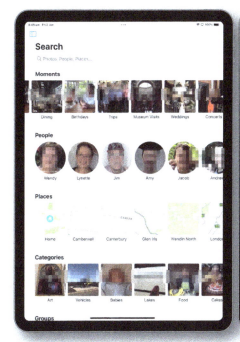 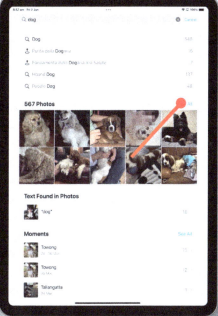

Most of the time, when you use the Search function, you will want to type in your own Search Phrase, into the search bar at the top.

As an example, if I type **dog** in that bar, the image above right shows the result.

If I want to see all the pictures that have been found, I tap **See All** to get a screen like that on right – from which I could choose **Select** at top right, and select some or all of the photos to, say, add to an Album.

Taking Photo of your Screen - Screenshots

How to take a Screenshot

Taking a photo of your device's screen can be so handy when you don't have access to a printer but need to keep a record of something that is on your iPad or iPhone screen.

For devices **with a Home Button**,

- Quickly press the **Sleep Switch** and the **Home Button** at the same time.

For devices **without a Home Button**

- Quickly press the **Sleep Switch** and **the Volume Up** buttons at the same time.

A small thumbnail of your screenshot will then appear at the bottom left of the screen. This thumbnail will disappear after a few seconds.

If it disappears, you can find it in your Photos library as the most Recent photo.

After you take a screenshot

Here's what you can do with that thumbnail while it is still on the screen.

- Swipe left on the thumbnail to get it off the screen (which saves it to your Photos library).
- Touch and hold the thumbnail to see the Share menu pop up and choose to share the screenshot.
- Tap it to add drawings or text to the screenshot (a feature called Markup). You may need to tap the pencil symbol at top see the Markup options at the bottom.

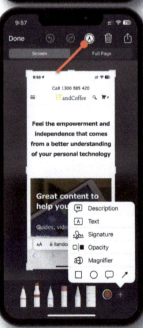

This feature is so handy when you need to send a photo to someone and highlight or point to something about that photo. Use any of the

Taking Photo of your Screen - Screenshots

pencils and other tools shown to add your annotations – which can include a signature, text and more.

When finished 'marking up' your photo, choose the **Share** symbol to share the photo – e.g. by email, Messages, Airdrop.

Or choose Done at top left to see a list of options, as shown in the image on the right. If the screenshot does not need to be retained, choose Delete Screenshot.

There is also a relatively new option, to Copy and Delete – allowing the screenshot to be copied to the clipboard (for pasting elsewhere) without retaining the screenshot in the Photos library.

Finding all those Screenshots

Your collection of Screenshots can be easily located (and managed – as we can end up with a lot that we don't need to keep!) from the **Media Types** area of the Photos app. (Refer page 17 for further information on where to locate this area/album.)

Live Text in Screenshots

In recent releases of iOS/iPadOS, a new feature has appeared for these Screenshots.

Where Markup mode is not currently active (tap the pencil at top right to exit Markup mode) you will see a bar at the bottom.

If there is any text in the image, this bar will show **Crop and scale or select text.**

Tap the **Live Text** symbol

Saving Photos from
Mail, Messages, Safari

Save to Photos from an email

A photo received in a mail message can be directly exported (saved to your Photos library).

Touch and hold on a photo in your mail message, then tap the **Save Image** option (or **Save n Images** if there are multiple images in the email) – as shown in the middle image below.

Alternatively, tap an individual image in the email to view that image (as shown in rightmost image above), and then choose the **Share** option (at bottom left on iPhone, top right on iPad) to see the list of options.

Scroll down to see the **Save Image** option (to save just this image to the Photos library).

Saving Photos from Mail, Messages, Safari

Save to Photos from Messages

If you receive a single photo or a set of photos in a Message, simply tap the 'down-arrow' on right of the image/s to save it/them to your Photos Library.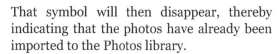

That symbol will then disappear, thereby indicating that the photos have already been imported to the Photos library.

If you receive several photos and they appear as a 'stack' of photos (as shown in the second set in the example on the right), swipe through the 'stack' of photos to view their thumbnails. If you see one you want to save, touch and hold and choose **Save**.

If you want to view the full photo (instead of just the thumbnail), tap the photo. If there were several, swipe right-to-left and vice-versa to scroll through them.

Then, for any you then wish to save to your Photos library, tap the Share symbol (bottom left on iPhone, top right on iPad) and choose **Save Photo** from list of options.

If you want to see all the photos that appear in a Messages conversation, tap the person's name at the top, then scroll down to the section headed **Photos** and choose **See All**.

You can then **Select** any photos from this set and choose the **Save** option that appears at bottom left, to save to the Photos library.

Saving Photos from Mail, Messages, Safari

Save Photos from a Web Page

Similarly, photos from a web page can also be saved to your Photos library.

Touch and hold on a web page's photo until some options appear, and (if it is available) choose the **Save to Photos** option.

Not all images you see on a web page can be saved – so you may not always see the **Save to Photos** option.

Finding the photos you just saved

You will then be able to find any photo/s that you add from other apps as the most recent in the **Recent** album.

These saved photos will also appear in the **Library**, but they may not be the last in the list – as their position in the Library timeline will depend on the Date Taken information that is recorded against the image, and whether that metadata is saved with the photo when it is exported from Safari.

Importing Photos

Importing from a Camera

Photos can be imported into to your iPad's or iPhone's Photos Library from a camera or its SD card. To do this, you need to purchase an accessory called a Camera Adaptor.

There are two types of Camera Adaptor – one that allows you to connect to the iPad/iPhone using the camera's USB cable, and the other that allows you to connect the camera's SD card to the iPad.

To import photos from your Camera, just plug in the camera's USB cord to the USB adaptor or take out the SD card and plug it into the SD adaptor.

Then plug the adaptor into your iPad or iPhone. (Or plug in the adaptor to the iPad/iPhone first – it doesn't matter!)

On the iPad, the Camera will show under a section called Devices in the left sidebar.

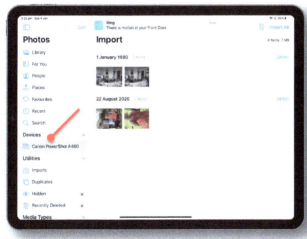

On the iPhone, a new option appears along the bottom of the screen – the **Import** option.

Touch on **Import** option (iPhone) or the camera name in the sidebar (iPad) to see thumbnails of all the photos that are on the camera or SD card.

Importing Photos

A green tick on any of the photos shows that the photo has already been imported onto this iPad/iPhone but has then been retained on camera/card.

Touch on **Import All** at the top right to import all photos that have not yet been imported.

Alternatively, tap on just those photos that you wish to import – a blue tick will show on the selected photos. Then tap **Import** (top right) and choose to **Import All** or just **Import Selected**.

Once importing of the photos is completed, you will have the option to **Delete** those that were imported from the camera/SD card or **Keep** them.

The photos that you just imported will be available in album called **Imports,** (which will only appear if you have done any importing) – see page 16 for where to find this album.

The imported photos will also appear in your Recent album, as the last photos in that album. In the Library view, they will appear on the timeline according to the Date Taken for each imported photo.

The **Photos** app and Camera Adaptor also give you the ability to delete some or all of the photos that are stored on the connected Camera or SD card.

Once again, touch on the **Import** option at the bottom right (iPhone) or the

Importing Photos

camera name in the sidebar (iPad). You will see the Delete All option at the top left - touch this to remove all the photos from the camera or SD card.

Confirm by touching the **Delete All** confirmation message.

Alternatively, tap on individual photos to give them a blue tick, then choose Delete at top left.

(NOTE: Touching on a photo that has a green tick will turn the tick to blue, to show that it has been specifically selected for the next action.)

Then touch on the red confirmation message to complete the deletion of those photos with blue ticks.

If you see an **Already Imported** heading like that shown in the example above right, tap Show All to see all the photos and then choose which to delete.

Importing photos from an external storage device

If you have images on another external storage device – for example, a USB stick or portable HDD (hard disk drive) you may be able to import this content to your iPad or iPhone.

Newer iPads allow the connection of a USB-C flash drive (i.e. USB stick) or, using an adaptor, a USB-A flash drive.

You can also purchase a USB stick that can plug into both a computer and an iPad or iPhone. Some will work on both iPad and/or iPhone on their own, others will require that there is an additional power source for the external device, which means you need a special adaptor that allow you to plug in a power source.

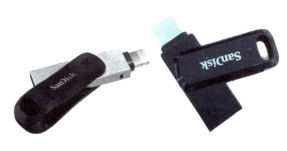

Importing Photos

Bigger portable HDDs will require a power source when plugged in to your iPhone/iPad – see examples on right.

When you plug in such a storage device, you will see a message pop up if the device does need extra power.

If the device is able to be read by the iPad or iPhone, you will see that device listed under **Locations** in the **Files** app.

Tap the device name in the sidebar to see its contents.

Select (using **Select** option at top right of Files) the images that you want to import, then choose **Share** at bottom left and **Save n Images** to import the selected photos/videos to the Photos library.

Note that certain external devices – like the example shown first on the previous page – may require the use of an App to transfer content back and forth between the devices.

If this is the case, the device won't appear in the Files app. You will need to check the instructions for the device to ascertain the details of the required app and how to use it.

Finding and Resolving Duplicates

It is certainly not unusual to find yourself with lots of duplicate photos in your Photos Library.

Up until iOS/iPadOS 16, there was no built-in feature for discovering and sorting out duplicates. Fortunately, this changed in 2022.

Apple has finally provided a feature that can detect and help you resolve the duplicated photos in your library. This new Duplicates view/album can locate exact copies (which have the same metadata), as well as photos that appear the same or similar.

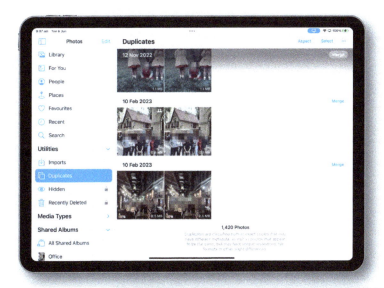

You can review the duplicates one-by-one and choose **Merge** to resolve the duplication.

The confirmation message that appears will depend on whether the photos are exact copies, or whether they

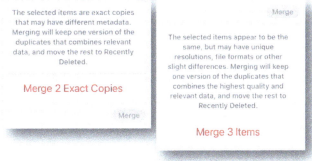

have different resolutions, formats, or other slight differences. See above message samples. Choose **Merge n Exact Copies** or **Merge n Items** to confirm.

Finding and Resolving Duplicates

Or you can choose to Select at top right, then Select All. Unselect any sets of photos you don't want to merge.

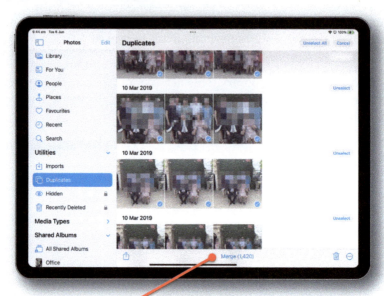

Tap the words **Merge (*nnn*)** at bottom of the screen (where nnn is the total number of photos selected) to perform the bulk merge.

A confirmation message will appear.

If it found a combination of exact copies AND others with different metadata, you will see a message like that on right – allowing the choice of whether to merge all, or just those that are copies.

Any photos confirmed as duplicates will be moved to the **Recently Deleted** album.

The great thing about this new feature is that any removal of duplicates will not impact your Albums – even if the photo in the album is the one being deleted. It will be replaced with the photo that is retained.

iCloud Photos

iCloud Photos was introduced in April 2015.

It provides centralised storage of all your photos in iCloud and allows the syncing, viewing, and updating of the Photos library in iCloud from any devices connected to that iCloud account.

There are now three aspects of iCloud that relate to your photos and videos.

iCloud Photos   Stores all your photos in iCloud and allows each of your devices to view and manage this same set of photos and Albums.

Extra iCloud storage may be needed to store large libraries, and devices that can't fit the entire library will Optimise content and may need internet access when to view the original version of photos. (Note. Windows computers can also use iCloud Photos.)

iCloud Shared Photo Library

New in iOS/iPadOS 16 is the **Shared Library** feature, allowing you to share a whole library of photos with up to 5 people. We have an extended description of this feature from page 112.

Shared Albums   Allows creation of albums in iCloud, albums that can be then shared with other people.

These Shared Albums are separate to your iCloud Photos – so deleting a photo from your library will not delete it from any Shared Album (and vice-versa) you have added it to.

If you use iCloud Photos, Shared Albums do not add to your iCloud storage usage. A Shared Album can have up to 5000 items in it.

Managing the various aspects of photos in iCloud is the done from: **Settings -> your-name -> iCloud -> Photos**. Enable iCloud photos by turning on **Sync this iPhone** (or iPad).

iCloud Photos

Note. A legacy feature called **My Photo Stream** has also existed since the inception of iCloud in 2011. This feature will be shut down in July 2023, so is not covered by this book.

Your Storage Options

Depending on the amount of storage available on your device, you can choose in your **Photos** Settings whether you wish to:

- **Download and Keep Originals** - to store all your photos and videos on your device as well as in iCloud. You will only be able to choose this option if you have sufficient storage on the device for your entire Photos library.

- **Optimise iPhone** *(or iPad)* **Storage** to reduce the storage used by your Photos library on this device by optimising it – storing reduced resolution versions of photos (which means viewing the full version of many photos and videos may require internet access).

The great benefits of iCloud Photos

There are many great reasons for using iCloud Photos:

- Photos and videos are synchronised between all devices that are connected to iCloud Photos. This means you have your photos and videos at your fingertips whenever you need them.

- Albums are synchronised - meaning that albums can be created on an iPhone, iPad, and Mac, and be visible then on all other devices.

- Folders you create in your Mac's Photos app (and now also in the iPad/iPhone app) are synchronized between all devices.

- The **Favourites** album synchronises.

- The **People** albums synchronise.

- Photos deleted on one device are also deleted on other devices.

- Photo edits are synchronized across devices.

- If your iPhone or iPad is lost – in fact, if all your devices are lost - your photos are safely stored and readily available in iCloud.

- You can view your photos from a web browser, by visiting iCloud.com.

iCloud Photos

For many people, this offers a great solution for storage of their photos and videos, allowing the Photos apps on iOS and MacOS to seamlessly manage your library of photos and videos. I do use this service on all my Apple devices and love it.

Sharing a Photos Library

iOS 16 and iPadOS 16 have finally brought us the Shared Library feature – offering another great benefit of iCloud Photos.

You can now set up an alternative library that you share with up to 5 other family members or close friends. You put all your photos into the shared library – so that the other person/people can see them all – or selectively choose the photos you want to go into that library.

This now offers a great way of collecting together all the family photos in one place, accessible by all who want to use and see them.

We'll cover this new feature in more detail shortly.

The disadvantages of iCloud Photos

The problems can start when your Photos library is a large one.

iCloud Photos offers only an 'all or nothing' solution to storage of your photos on each device.

This means that, if iCloud Photos is turned on, the device will show EVERY photo and video that is in the iCloud library. You don't get to choose to selectively sync only certain albums to your Apple mobile devices and Mac.

Inability to access photos without internet

If your library is big, it may not fit on your iPad or iPhone.

In this case, your device will store 'cut down' versions of some or all your photos and videos – which means photos may be blurry and only able to be viewed properly once they are downloaded from your iCloud.

Videos may take a while to download and play, again using up internet download data (perhaps your mobile data).

This is referred to as **Optimised** storage of your Photos and Videos, where not all photos and videos in your Photos library are stored on your device. The thumbnail of the photo/video will show, but the photo/video itself may need to be downloaded from your iCloud.

iCloud Photos

You need internet access to view the **Optimised** photos and videos and usually must endure a delay before you can see full resolution versions of your photos and videos.

Unexpected Mobile Data Use

This can result in unexpected mobile data usage, and great frustration at the delay in seeing a clear image, or at not being able to view photos and videos when there is no internet.

Added costs of iCloud Photos

I have chosen with my more recent iPhones to purchase larger capacity iPhones (i.e. at least 256GB) so that I can 'download and keep' my entire 160GB Photos library.

This, of course, means I paid a higher price for my device. Added to all this is the cost of storing all my photos and videos in iCloud, as I need to pay for the 200GB storage plan (at $4.49 per month).

Once you exceed your 5GB free storage limit for iCloud (which most people do if they use iCloud Backup and/or iCloud Photos), you must start paying for your iCloud storage.

Your computer says there are no photos to import

We regularly see clients with this problem after they have (often accidentally) turned on iCloud Photos.

If you turn on iCloud Photos on an iPhone or iPad that has a relatively small amount of storage, you can find that you are no longer able to just plug your iPad/iPhone into your computer and import new photos/videos to that device.

You may be told that there are no photos/videos on your iPhone/iPad.

This is because your photos have been uploaded to iCloud, and only optimised versions of the photos have been left on the iPhone/iPad. These optimised versions cannot be imported to the computer.

You are left wondering where your Photos have gone, and how to get them onto your computer if you don't want to use iCloud Photos.

We look at options for resolving this problem in our books **The Comprehensive Guide to iCloud** and the **Introduction to the Mac – The Photos App**.

iCloud Photos

Should you use iCloud Photos?

The benefits of iCloud Photos, as described earlier, are huge.

But iTandCoffee's recommendation is that you don't set up iCloud Photos unless you are fully aware of the implications and have the storage space to store your whole library on at least one of your devices – or are happy to accept that not all your photos/videos will be available to look at straight away and that you will need internet to access them.

If iCloud Photos has been accidentally enabled, it can be tricky to undo. And you can find some unexpected consequences of turning this feature on and off.

Turning off iCloud Photos

You can turn off iCloud Photos by turning of the **Sync this iPhone** (or **iPad**) in **Settings->*your-name*-> iCloud->Photos**

If you have sufficient space to store your Photos library on your device and you have selected to **Download and Keep Original**, turning off iCloud Photos should leave all photos and videos on your device.

In fact, it is a good idea to turn on this option and try to download all the photos to your device before you turn off iCloud Photos (assuming that you want to keep all those photos on that device).

If your device has had the **Optimise Storage** option selected, some or all the photos on your device could be low resolutions versions.

If there are any such photos on your device, turning off iCloud Photos (by turning off the iCloud Photos option in your settings/preferences) will require that you agree to remove these low-resolution photos/videos from your device.

These items will still be available in your iCloud and can be viewed at icloud.com.

iCloud Shared Library

Share a Photos Library with family and/or friends

As mentioned above, iOS/iPadOS 16 now allows the set up a central Shared Library that can be seen and used by up to 5 other family members and/or friends.

You can only participate in one Shared library. Typically, this will be a Family shared library that all members of the family can use. And the person who creates the Shared Library must have sufficient iCloud storage for all participants. The photos in the Shared Library do not count towards participants' iCloud allowance.

For collections of photos that you share with different groups of people, Shared iCloud Albums are still available (see next section).

Create an iCloud Shared Photo Library

To get started, go to **Settings -> your- name -> iCloud -> Photos -> Shared Library** and tap **Shared Library**, then **Get Started**

You will first need to choose the family member/s or friend/s with whom you wish to share new library. Choose **Add Participant** to select one or more participants. Type in the Apple ID (i.e. email address), mobile number or name of the person you wish to invite, then choose **Add** at top right (or choose to **Add Later** at bottom to choose participants later)

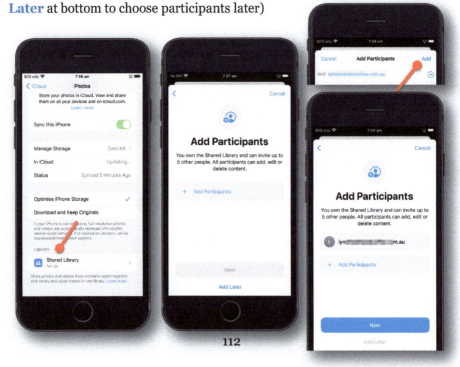

iCloud Shared Library

You can then add further Participants. It is important to note that you can only share with someone who is an Apple iCloud user, and who has chosen to use iCloud Photos. They must also be using iOS/iPadOS 16.

Once you have finished choosing the Participants, choose **Next** (see final image on previous page).

You will then be asked to choose how you wish to populate the new Shared Library.

You can choose to share ALL your current photos and videos, choose certain people or a date range, or choose to manually select the photos to share (see image on right).

I recommend choose the **Move Photos Later** option (see bottom of screen on right) at this point – so that you can be more selective about which photos to add to this shared library.

Next you will be given the chance share the invitation to join the Shared Library with those you have chosen (see left image on right). This can be done by sending them a Message (choose **Invite via Messages** button), or by choosing the **Copy Link** option at bottom left.

You will then have the option to choose whether photos you take using the Camera on the device should go into the Shared Library automatically, or whether you want to pick

iCloud Shared Library

and choose what goes there.

The final screen in the setup process gives you some tips about using your Shared Library.

If you receive a Shared Library invitation ...

If you are the recipient of an invitation to share an iCloud Shared Photos Library, you will see the below left screen when you tap the link.

Choose **Get Started**, then choose which photos you wish to add to that library. I suggest that, at this point, you choose the **Move Photos Later** option at bottom).

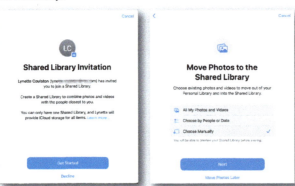

If you did select some photos to add to the library, you will get a Preview option (as shown in rightmost image above). Choose to preview or choose **Skip** if you don't need to do this.

You will then see the final confirmation screen, allowing you to confirm that you wish to **Join Shared Library**.

This confirmation shows the details of the Apple ID that you are joining as, and the number of photos you have chosen to move to the Shared Library initially.

You next see the screen on right, asking if you want photos shared from your iPhone's (and iPad's) Camera.

iCloud Shared Library

Again here, I recommend choosing **Share Manually Only**, so that you have some control over what ends up in the Shared Library.

The final screen in the setup series confirms that your Shared Library is ready (same as that shown earlier).

Select **Done** to exit the setup process.

Manage Shared Library Settings

Future management of the Shared Library can be done by the creator of the library by returning to **Settings -> your-name -> iCloud -> Photos -> Shared Library** – or from **Settings -> Photos -> Shared Library**

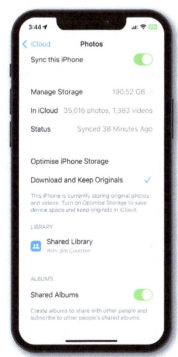
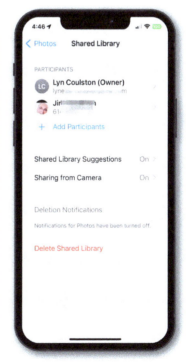

You can **Add Participants** (up to a total of 5), add photos of selected People, adjust some other settings and, if needed **Delete Shared Library** (as long as you are the person who created the Shared Library).

iCloud Shared Library

If you do choose the Delete option, you will be asked what you want to do with the photos that are in the Shared Library – to **Keep Everything** or **Keep only what I contributed**. Whatever you choose to keep will be then added to your personal library.

Choosing which Photos Library to View.

On the iPhone and iPad, tap ••• at top right to choose which Library you wish to view.

As you can see, the choice can be made to see all photos regardless of library (**Both Libraries**), or to choose to view just the **Personal Library** or just the **Shared Library**.

The **Shared Library Badge** option, if ticked, will mean that any photo that is in the Shared library will show the 'people' badge at top right, as shown in the example on the right.

Add Photos to the Shared Library

Make sure you are viewing either **Both Libraries** or **Personal Library**.

Select one or more photo thumbnails and then choose ••• at bottom right.

When viewing an individual photo, tap that same symbol at top right.

This provides the option to **Move to Shared Library**. Tap this to complete the move.

Alternatively, touch and hold on an individual photo's thumbnail to see same option.

iCloud Shared Library

Move your photos back to Personal Library

When you are viewing the Shared Library, follow the same process as defined above and choose the **Move to Personal Library** to move a photo (or selected set of photos) back to your own library. This can only be done for photos that you owned initially.

Automatically add photos to Shared Library

You can set up your iPhone and iPad to automatically (or manually) populate the Shared Library when a photo is taken.

The relevant options are found in the Settings app.

Go to **Settings -> *your-name* -> iCloud -> Photos -> Shared Library** or **Settings -> Camera-> Shared Library** to enable or disable **the Sharing from Camera** option.

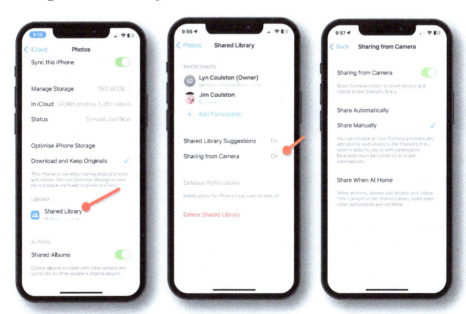

The rightmost image above shows the options available for sharing photos from the device's camera.

My own preference is to **Share Manually** and turn off **Share When at Home**, as I only want certain photos to go into the Shared Library.

Sharing Albums of Photos

Sharing Albums using iCloud

A set of photos can be shared with anyone, by using your iCloud and setting up **Shared Albums**.

Shared Albums allow you to share a set of photos with other iCloud users, AS WELL AS with other 'non-Apple' people – without using any additional iCloud storage allocation.

Shared Albums can have up to 5000 photos or videos.

I use iCloud Shared Albums all the time to share photos of trips, family events and more.

Those who share the album with you can like, comment, or even add more photos to the Shared Album. They can also download the photos for their own use.

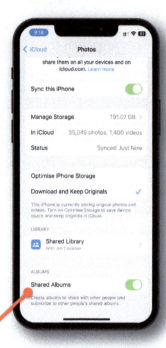

For this option to be available on your iPad or iPhone, you must ensure turn on the **Shared Album** feature from **Settings -> your-name -> iCloud -> Photos**.

Create or update a Shared Album

Having ensured that your Shared Albums option is active, it is then easy to share a set of photos via your iCloud.

- **Select** one or more photos (using the selection technique described earlier) – this can be from any thumbnail view.

- Choose the **Share** symbol

- Choose the option **Add to Shared Albums**

If you have never used a Shared Album before ...

- Enter a name for your Album, then choose **Next** (see first image on next page).

118

Sharing Albums of Photos

- Enter the Apple ID/s of the person or people you wish to share with – or just skip this step at this point. Either way, choose **Create** to go to the next step.

- Optionally provide a **Comment** about the photos that you are sharing (for others to see), then choose **Post** to complete creation of the Shared Album.

If you have previously used a Shared Album (viewed, created, updated, etc.) ...

- The screen will show the last **Shared Album** you worked with.

- If that is the correct Album, choose Post to add the photos to the Shared Album. You can first optionally add a **Comment** about the photos, one that the others who share the Shared Album will see.

- If the Shared Album shown is not the correct one – or if you would like to create a **New Shared Album** - tap on that album name to see the **Add to** screen (see image on right).

- Tap the applicable **Shared Album** if you wish to add to the album, then < to go back to previous screen and Post the photos to the selected Shared Album (after adding a Comment, if required).

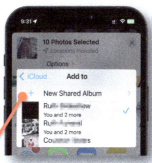

- Alternatively, choose **New Shared Album** to create a new Album – then follow the steps shown above for creating and sharing that new album.

Sharing Albums of Photos

Receiving an invitation to share a Shared Album

If you are invited to share a Shared Album, a red '1' will appear on the Photos app — indicating a notification sharing.

You may also see a notification about the share appear at the top each of your Apple devices (if Notifications for the Photos app are enabled) — as shown below.

To see what has been shared with you, tap the **For You** option (bottom bar on iPhone, side bar on iPad) to see the invitation and **Accept** or **Decline** it (see example on right).

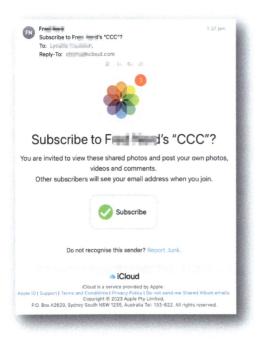

If you tap **Accept**, the Album will then be available to view in your **Shared Albums** area — i.e. you will be subscribed to that album.

You will also receive an email about the share (see example on left), offering the **Subscribe** option (which you can choose from this email if you haven't already accepted).

This is the same as **Accept**ing the invitation from the **For You** area, adding that album to your Shared Albums list.

Sharing Albums of Photos

Viewing Shared Albums

You can then view your Shared Albums – those that you have shared and that have been shared with you - as follows:

- On the iPhone, in the **Albums** area – scroll down to see the **Shared Albums** section and tap **See All** to see all your Shared Albums.

- On the iPad, in the **Shared Albums** section of the Sidebar. You will see an **All Shared Albums** option, as well as each of the Shared Albums listed under that. (If you don't see your list of Shared Albums, tap the **>** to expand that section.)

 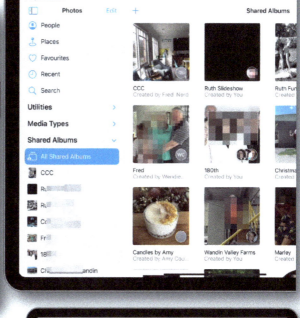

The **For You** area shows **Shared Album Activity** – reflecting the albums you recently joined or Shared, as well as any comments, additions, etc from others in relation to Shared Albums.

Sharing Albums of Photos

Saving photos from an Album shared with you

Photos in Shared Albums that have been shared by other people will not appear in your Library or Recent - and they will disappear if the Shared Album is deleted by the owner, or you 'unsubscribe' from it (see later in this section).

If you wish to permanently save other peoples' photos that you see in a Shared Albums area, you need to **Select** them and **Save** them to your Photos library.

Go to the **Shared Album** containing the photos you want to keep (see previous page for where to find your Shared Albums), then choose **Select** at top right to tap and select the photos you wish to keep.

Then choose the **Share** symbol and tap **Save Image** (for individual image) or **Save n Images** if multiple images are selected (as indicated in image on right). Your photos will then appear in the **Recent** album as the most recently added, and in the **Library** view according to the Date Taken of each photo.

To save ALL images from a Shared Album to your Photos library, tap ... at top right and choose **Share Photos**.

All of the photos in the Album will be selected, allowing you to then scroll down and choose **Save n Images**.

Adding photos or videos to a Shared Album

To add new photos to a Shared Album, go to the Shared Album and tap the +, or tap ... at top right and choose **Add Photos**.

Tap the photos you wish to add, from the Recent thumbnails shown - or choose Albums (along top) to view and select photos from other groupings.

Sharing Albums of Photos

Alternatively (and this is my own preferred method), use the same method described earlier – of selecting the photos first, then choosing the **Share** symbol and the **Add to Shared Album** option.

Follow the steps described on page 118 to select the applicable Shared Album and post the photos there.

Managing who shares your Album

Add new subscribers to a Shared Album at any time by choosing the 'Person' symbol at top right of the Shared Album you are viewing.

If you are the owner/creator of the Shared Album (i.e. the person who did the sharing), the screen below left will appear – allowing additional people to be invited to share the Album, or for previously invited people/subscribers to be removed.

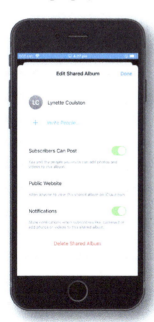

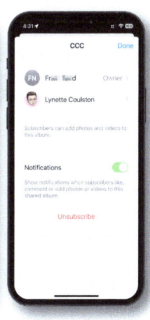

If you are not the owner, the rightmost screen above will appear – allowing you to see the list of other subscribers, to turn off **Notifications** for this Shared Album, or **Unsubscribe** from the Album (which we will cover shortly).

Sharing Albums of Photos

If you are the owner of the Album, tap **+ Invite People** to invite additional people to subscribe to the Album.

Also as owner, if there is someone you want to remove as a subscriber, tap on their name and choose **Remove Subscriber** (see middle image above)

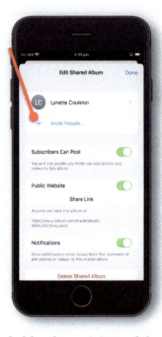

You will see several other options on the **Edit Shared Album** screen (leftmost above).

- **Subscribers Can Post** - Choose whether subscribers can add photos to the Shared Album

- **Public Website** – to allow non-Apple people to view your Shared Album. This generates a link to a web page that will show your Shared Album's photos, a link that can then be shared with those who don't use Apple or iCloud. Photos viewed in this way can then be downloaded by the recipient of the link. Choose **Share Link** to share the created link with others. (Note that the recipients of the link will not be listed in the 'subscriber' list, as anyone with this link can view the shared photos.)

- **Notifications** - Choose whether you want **Notifications** popping up on your iPad/iPhone about any activity in relation to the Shared Album.

Change the name of a Shared Album

To change the name of a Shared Album, tap ••• at top right when viewing the thumbnails of the Shared Album's photos.

You will see a long list of options, one of which is **Rename Album**. Tap and enter a new name for the Album.

Sharing Albums of Photos

All subscribers will then see the name of that Shared Album change in their own Photos library.

Unsubscribing from a Shared Album

If you no longer wish to see a Shared Album that someone else shared with you, just tap and choose **Unsubscribe**.

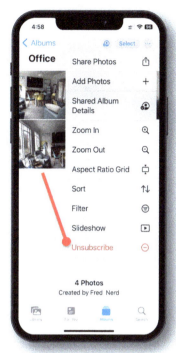

This will remove the album from the **Shared Albums** area on all your devices. Any photos that you didn't save to your own library will then be gone.

As we saw above, the **Unsubscribe** option is also found by tapping at 👥 top right when viewing the Shared Album.

Deleting a Shared Album

If you no longer want to keep a Shared Album that you created, tap ⋯ and choose **Delete Album** (see last image on previous page).

Alternatively, tap 👥 and choose the **Delete Shared Album** option (see the first image on the previous page).

The Shared Album will be removed from the Shared Albums area on all your own devices and will also disappear on any Subscriber's device.

The original photos used to populate the Shared Album will remain in the owner's Photo's library (unless any of those originals have already been deleted from the library).

What happens if Shared photos are deleted from library?

If you have shared an album of photos, and then delete any of those photos from the Photos library, the deleted photos will still appear in the Shared Album.

It is only if you delete that Shared Album that those photos will no longer be available.

Photos Settings

We have already touched on several of the **Settings** for the Photos app in earlier sections. But let's take a closer look at what you see in **Settings -> Photos**.

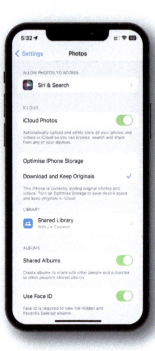

Siri & Search

As described when you tap this option, it will *'Allow information from "Photos" to appear in Search, Look Up and Keyboard. Siri may learn from and make suggestions based on how you use this app.'*

iCloud Photos, Optimise iPhone Storage, Download and Keep Originals, Shared Library, and Shared Albums

These options all match the options found in **Settings – your-name -> iCloud – Photos**, providing an alternative way of looking at and managing these options - described on pages 105-108.

Use Face ID (or Use Touch ID or Use Passcode)

With iOS/iPadOS 16, the **Recently Deleted** and **Hidden** Albums are able to be protected by your device's Face ID, Touch ID or passcode. This is to protect this potentially sensitive content from prying eyes. But if you don't want this feature enabled, turn off this option (described further on page 31).

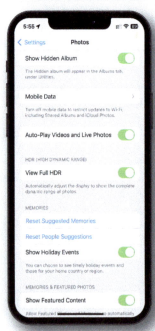

Show Hidden Album

There is a special album called the **Hidden** album, in which photos can be hidden so that they no longer appear in other views/albums (see page 29). If you want to be ultra-secretive, this Hidden album can be hidden from the Photos library so that it does not appear under **Utilities.** (Although this makes it impossible to see any photos you hide from within the Photos app – unless you return to this Setting and turn on this **Show Hidden Album** option.

Photos Settings

Mobile Data

This option allows you to decide if you want to use your **Mobile Data** for updating your iCloud Photos and your Shared Albums, and then whether you want to allow **Unlimited Updates**. I tend to leave both of these options turned off so that I don't waste my mobile data – unless I am going to be away from Wi-Fi for a while and need my new photos to be sync'd – in which case I turn on **Mobile Data**, but leave **Unlimited Updates** turned off.

Auto-play Videos and Live Photos

If you would prefer that videos do not start automatically, and that Live Photos do not play as a video when you are swiping through and viewing individual photos and videos.

View Full HDR (only visible on certain devices)

HDR is a feature that can automatically balance lighting and exposure for your photos to give you a better photo - to "*Automatically adjust the display to show the complete dynamic range of photos*". Leave on (if available) for the best effect.

Reset Suggested Memories and Reset People Suggestions

In the Photos app, you can select options to request that particular memories or people are featured less. The 'Reset' option you see in Settings will allow previously blocked places, dates, holidays, or people to be included in new Memories.

Show Holiday Events

This setting determines whether your Photos app will present Memories that are based on the Holiday events that apply to your country.

Show Featured Content

If you don't want Featured Phots and Memories to automatically appear in **For You** in Photos or in Widgets, turn this setting off.

Transfer to Mac or PC

When you transfer your device's photos to a computer, they can retain the format they had on the iPhone or iPad (the **Keep Originals** option), or they can be automatically converted into a format that is compatible with the computer you are transferring to (the **Automatic** option). (I keep this set to **Automatic**.)

Transferring Photos To Your Computer

Transferring of Photos from your iPad or iPhone to your computer can be achieved in a few ways.

- Transfer via USB cable
- iCloud Photos
- Third-party cloud storage solutions like Dropbox, OneDrive, or Google Photos.
- Airdropping from iPhone/iPad to Mac
- Using an external storage device that is compatible with iPad/iPhone AND the computer.

This guide will not aim to cover all of these in detail, as the focus here is on the features of the Photos app of your iPad and iPhone. We will look just at the first option – transfer via USB cable.

An important thing to realise is that, when you plug your iPad or iPhone into your computer using its USB cable, your computer will recognise that your iPad or iPhone as a camera.

So, your computer will activate whatever process it would normally activate when a camera is plugged in.

But please note that, if you use iCloud Photos, you may find that there are no photos to import to your computer – if the photos on the iPad or iPhone are optimised and therefore not downloaded.

Transferring photos to a Mac

On a Mac, you will normally want to import your photos/videos to the Photos app (assuming iCloud Photos is not turned on and already syncing your photos. When your iPad or iPhone is plugged to the Mac in via USB, the device will appear in the sidebar of the Photos app on the Mac, ready for you to choose what photos/videos to import.

Refer to iTandCoffee's book **Introduction to the Mac – The Photos App** for more details of how to import photos to the Mac's Photos App.

Another alternative for importing photos is available on the Mac.

Transferring Photos to your Computer

An app called **Image Capture** allows you to import some of all of the photos to your computer to a USB Stick or an external portable hard drive.

This would be something to consider using if you really don't want to put the photos into your Photos library - for example, if the photos belong to someone else and you are putting them onto an external storage drive for them.

We won't go into how to use this app as part of this guide – check out tips on the iTandCoffee website for further information.

Transferring iPad and iPhone photos to your Windows Computer

On Windows, an AutoPlay window will normally pop up when you plug in your iPad or iPhone using the USB cable. (Note that the examples below are from Windows 10.)

This will give you options for importing the pictures onto your computer.

Click on either of the first two options (depending on your preference) and follow the prompts to import your photos.

Alternatively, open Windows Explorer and look for the **My Computer** area on the left side. You should see your iPhone or iPad listed in that area.

Right-click on the device name, and choose the **Import Pictures and videos option.**

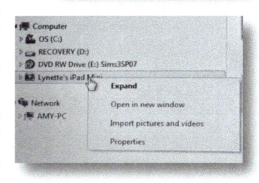

This will then start the same process as that described above.

If you want to manage the importing of photos and videos manually – rather than using the 'Import photos and videos' wizard – you can also do this from Windows Explorer.

Transferring Photos to your Computer

Once again you need to find your device in the My Computer section of the left sidebar and click on the iPad/iPhone that appears there. Look for the **DCIM folder** (found under the folder called **Internal Storage**).

This folder will hold sub-folders that contain photos on your iPhone or iPad, each usually relating to a particular date range.

You can then manually move whole folders of photos, or sets of photos within folders, using standard file management techniques on Windows.

Transfer to external storage device then to computer

There is also the option to save photos from your iPad's Photos library to an external storage device – if you have a compatible external storage device and any necessary accessory (as described on page 103).

When you have selected a set of photos in the Photos app, the Share option will also provide the option to **Save to Files**.

If a compatible external device is plugged in, you will see this device listed under Locations in the 'save as' screen provided for Files.

Tap this device to see the content – and tap any sub-folder you see to go to that sub-folder (if you want to save to a sub-folder).

When you are located in the required folder, choose **Save** at top right.

You will then be able to plug that device into the computer and import the photos you have just saved there.

Transferring photos from a computer

If you don't use iCloud Photos (or just don't want to use it on your computer), transferring of photos from your computer to your iPhone or iPad can be achieved in several ways, including (but not limited to)

- **iCloud Photos** - If you don't want to turn on iCloud Photos on your computer, you can sign in to iCloud.com and upload the computer's photos to your iCloud. If your iPad and iPhone are using iCloud Photos, the photos you upload will magically appear.

- Creating a **Shared Album** on your Mac that you can then see on your iPad and iPhone and saving the photos to your device's library from there.

- **Airdropping** – if you have a Mac.

- **Syncing photos** – create an album/albums or folder/folders of photos on your computer, then use the Photos tab in then use the iTunes or Finder app (depending on what computer and operating system you are using) to choose albums/folders for syncing. (We won't go into this one further here.)

- **Transfer via an external storage device** - See page 103 for how to import from such a device.

For more information about and assistance with any of the above options, please consult iTandCoffee.

Related books by iTandCoffee

The following books by iTandCoffee are mentioned throughout this book:

- Introduction to the iPad and iPhone – A Guided Tour

- Introduction to the Mac – The Photos App

- The Comprehensive Guide to iCloud

To obtain a copy of any of these books – in either paperback or digital format - visit the iTandCoffee Online Store at

www.itandcoffee.com.au/store